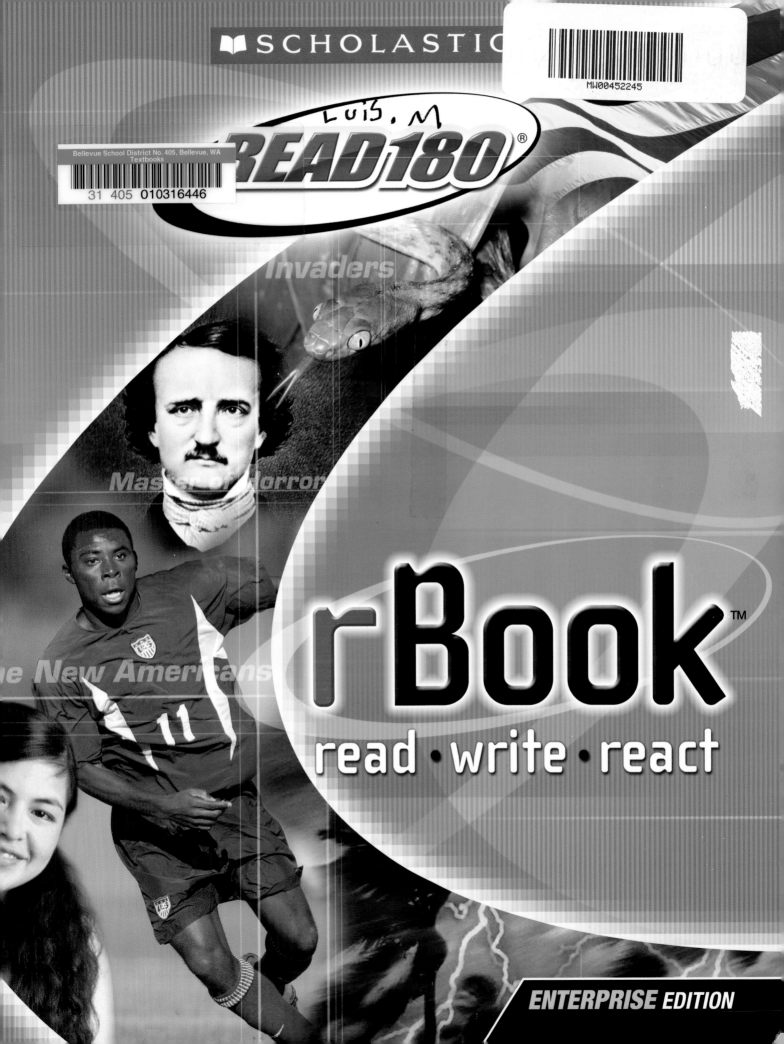

SCHOLASTIC

READ 180 ®

Invaders

Master of Horror

The New Americans

rBook™
read · write · react

ENTERPRISE EDITION

BELLEVUE TITLE I

READ 180®

rBook™

Stage B

Table of Contents

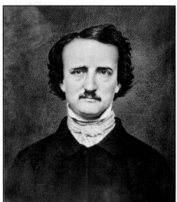

Nonfiction and Literature

The Streets of Harlem

Welcome to the rBook

Get ready for the rBook by taking this quiz. After you finish each Workshop, check back to see if your ideas or opinions have changed.

1 The New Americans

Read each statement below. Write *A* if you agree. Write *D* if you disagree.

_A_ Anyone in the world should be allowed to live in the U.S.

_A_ All newcomers to America should learn to speak English.

_d_ Sports stars from other countries, like Freddy Adu, should be put at the top of the list to become new U.S. citizens.

2 When Disaster Strikes

A hurricane is heading your way. Read the following statements. Check the one you think is right.

❑ You should stay in your home and keep your family, property, and pets safe.

❑ You should leave your house and go with your family to a shelter.

3 Identity Crisis

Imagine that you can choose your own identity. Decide which choice you would make. Circle it.

1. I would stay exactly who I am.

2. I would get a new life with new parents and new friends.

3. I would change some things about myself and keep other things the same.

4 Stolen Childhoods

Think about the Workshop title, "Stolen Childhoods." Look at the photos below. What do you predict this Workshop will be about?

_____

_____

_____

5 Under Pressure

Are teens under pressure? Check the three pressures that you think are the worst for teens today.

____ pressure to be a good kid

____ pressure to smoke

____ pressure to work hard at school

____ pressure to look good

____ pressure to fit in with friends

____ pressure to earn money

6 Poe: The Master of Horror

Edgar Allan Poe wrote many creepy stories, including "The Fall of the House of Usher." Look at the picture of the house below. Who do you think might live there? Check one.

☐ a creepy family with coffins in the basement

☐ a weird horror-story writer

☐ a rich vampire from Europe

☐ a clan of creatures from another world

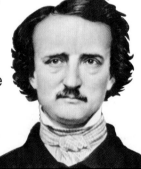

7 Alien Invaders

Check out the Chinese snakehead fish at right. It's an alien invader. What kinds of problems might it cause?

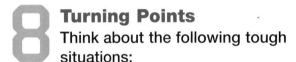

_____

_____

_____

_____

_____

8 Turning Points

Think about the following tough situations:

☐ moving to a new country

☐ struggling with a serious illness

☐ finding out that a parent has gone to jail

Which situation do you think would be the toughest for a teen to face? Check your answer.

9 The Streets of Harlem

Author Walter Dean Myers grew up in Harlem. Sometimes, he got into trouble. Then he had to decide what to do about it. How do you handle trouble? Read each statement. Write **A** if you agree. Write **D** if you disagree.

____ If I do something wrong, I don't admit it until I have to.

____ I think honesty is always the best policy.

____ If I get into trouble, I go to my parents for help.

____ I think that a little lie never hurt anybody.

WORKSHOP 1

NONFICTION

Comprehension Focus
Main Idea and Details

READINGS
1 *School Before Soccer* >> Newspaper Article
2 *Fitting In* >> Profile
3 *A New Immigration Boom* >> Social Studies Text

The NEW Americans

Where do Americans come from? They come from all over the world. They come from China, Mexico, Europe, India, and Africa. America has always been a home for newcomers.

Why do so many people come here? Some want an education. Some want jobs. Everyone wants freedom and a better life.

Get ready to meet some new Americans. Find out how their lives have changed here. Find out how they are changing America.

VOCABULARY BUILDER

Target Word ⊙	Meaning	Example
▶ Read the Target Words. Rate each one using the scale below.*	▶ Read the Target Word meanings. Write in the missing ones.	▶ Finish the Target Word examples below. Write in the missing ones.
communicate com•mu•ni•cate *(verb)* ① ② ③		*I communicate with my friends by using . . .*
immigrant im•mi•grant *(noun)* ① ② ③	*a person who moves from one country to another country*	
influence in•flu•ence *(verb)* ① ② ③		My friend **influences** me to study more.
policy pol•i•cy *(noun)* ① ② ③	*a rule*	
trend trend *(noun)* ① ② ③		*Examples of trends at my school are . . .*

*Rating Scale
① = I don't know it at all.
② = I've seen it before.
③ = I know it and use it.

School Before Soccer
Young Soccer Star Graduates

Freddy Adu in action on the soccer field.

May 5, 2005—Freddy Adu is a hot new soccer star. He's only 15, but already he plays for a pro team. It's a lot for a teen to handle. Yet for Freddy, school—not soccer—always came first.

Freddy's family moved to America from Ghana when he was eight. His parents wanted a better education for their kids.

In the U.S., Freddy worked hard at school. But he missed playing soccer with his friends. One day, Freddy was practicing. A classmate saw him play. He asked Freddy to join his soccer team. Soon, Freddy became their star player.

Freddy's fame grew. Large crowds came to his games. An Italian team even made Freddy an offer. They wanted to pay him $750,000 to play!

Then Freddy's mom stepped in. She reminded Freddy why they came to America. Her words influenced him. Freddy rejected the team's offer. He focused on school instead. He studied hard enough to graduate early.

Freddy found a way to play soccer and finish school. He graduated last year—at age 14! He also joined his hometown pro team. **Currently**, Freddy plays for the D.C. United. Both of Freddy's dreams —school and soccer— have come true. **END**

Words to Know! **rejected** turned down

Main Idea and Details

The **main idea** is the most important point about a topic. **Details** are the facts that support the main idea. To find the main idea and details:

- Decide what the topic is. Find the main idea about the topic.
- Look for the details that support the main idea.

▶ **Fill in this chart with the main idea and details of "School Before Soccer."**

Detail

Freddy is very talented at soccer.

Detail

Main Idea

Detail

Detail

Write What is this article mainly about?

_____

_____

_____

VOCABULARY BUILDER
Target Word

income

in•come (noun)

Rate it: ① ② ③

Meaning

_____

_____

Example

_____

_____

_____

 React

Moving was hard for Irene. Should she have stayed in Mexico with her grandmother? Why or why not?

Irene Rodriguez, 18, is an immigrant from Mexico. She now lives in Los Angeles.

FITTING IN

by Jonathan Blum

It's hard to fit in when you're new in school. It's *really* hard to fit in when you're new in the country, too!

Imagine moving to a new country. You don't know your way around. You feel isolated and sad. You can't even communicate. But your parents still expect you to succeed. That's how it was for Irene Rodriguez. This young immigrant turned failure into success.

Leaving Mexico

Irene was born in a small Mexican town. When Irene was young, her dad worked 12 hours a day. But his **income** was still too small to support a family. Finally, Irene's dad moved to Los Angeles for better pay. "I didn't see him for five years," Irene says.

When Irene was nine, her family decided to join her dad. They moved to L.A., where they hoped to find a better life.

Even though life in Mexico was hard, leaving was even harder. Irene's grandmother stayed behind. "I remember leaving her," Irene says. "She cried and waved good-bye. It was so hard to look back and see her. She was getting smaller and smaller."

Strange New World

Los Angeles was a big change from Mexico. There were bright lights and tall buildings everywhere. Cars clogged the streets and noise filled the air. "I felt like I was in another world," Irene says. "I was lost."

Back home in Mexico, Irene had spent a lot of time outside. "You could ride your bike," Irene remembers. "You didn't worry that a car was going to run you over." ➡

Main Idea and Details

1. **Write** ▷ Find the main idea in the section "Leaving Mexico."

_____

_____

_____

_____

_____

2. **Write** ▷ Find the main idea in the section called "Strange New World."

_____

_____

_____

_____

_____

3. **Underline** ▷ Find two important details that support the main idea in "Strange New World."

Active Reading

Underline ▸ What advice does Irene have for new immigrants?

VOCABULARY BUILDER
Target Word

motivate

mo•ti•vate (verb)

Rate it: ① ② ③

Meaning

_____

_____

Example

_____

_____

_____

 React

Write ▸ Who had an easier time adjusting to the U.S.—Irene or Freddy Adu? Why?

_____

_____

_____

_____

_____

_____

_____

_____

Starting Over

Starting school was a struggle for Irene, too. She didn't know English. "It was frustrating," she says. "I didn't understand what people were saying."

Irene *really* hated writing in English. "Every time I wrote something, I thought people were laughing at me," she says.

Then, a bad report card made things even worse. Irene got two F's and a D. Her dad was really angry. "I'm not sending you to school to get this type of grade," he told her. Irene got the message. Her father's words **motivated** her to learn English fast.

A Plan for Success

Irene came up with a plan. She had a friend in her English as a Second Language (ESL) class. Together, they agreed to communicate with each other only in English. "When we got stuck, we

Irene works with friends on the computer.

> "Try something new," Irene says. "It will make you a better person."

said the word in Spanish," Irene says. "But we kept everything else in English."

By high school, Irene's policy of hard work had paid off. She communicated well in English. She got better grades. She even assisted other ESL students.

Irene knows how hard it is to fit in. She has advice for new immigrants. "Try something new," Irene says. "It will make you a better person." *END*

Words to Know! **assisted** helped

Main Idea and Details

▶ Fill in this chart with the main idea and details in "Fitting In."

Detail

_____

_____

_____

_____

Detail

_____

_____

_____

_____

Main Idea

_____

_____

_____

_____

Detail

_____

_____

_____

_____

Detail

_____

_____

_____

_____

A New Immigration BOOM

A new wave of immigrants is coming to America. Find out how they are influencing our nation.

The U.S. Census

In 2000, the U.S. census counted Americans. There were 281,421,906 of us. How do we know? Our government sent millions of forms to homes. Most families responded by mail. Door-to-door workers tried to find everyone else. Then, everyone was counted. The census happens every ten years—and it teaches us a lot.

The census doesn't just count heads. It helps Americans _understand_ America. The census asks important questions. Where were people born? What languages do they speak? When did they move here? What are their jobs?

Since 1790, census records have kept track of Americans. If you look at past records, you can see how America has changed. You can see immigration trends.

New citizens attend their swearing-in ceremony.

The New Immigrants

Where have new Americans come from? Immigration trends have changed over time. In the past, U.S. policies made it easier for people from Europe to immigrate. Up until 1965, most immigrants came from Europe. In contrast, only a **minimum** number of Asians and Latinos were allowed to immigrate. Most were rejected.

Then, in 1965, the law changed. It made immigration more fair. Soon after, a new immigration trend began. Newcomers from Asia and Latin America started settling across the country. They brought their food, music, and cultures with them.

Latino culture is having an especially big impact on our nation. Burritos are catching up with hamburgers as America's favorite food. Latino musicians sell millions of records. There are more Spanish magazines and TV shows. The census numbers help explain why.

Words to Know! **impact** effect

📖 **Main Idea and Details**

1. ⟨Write⟩ Find the main idea in the section "The U.S. Census."

_____

_____

_____

_____

_____

_____

_____

2. ⟨Underline⟩ Find two important details in "The U.S. Census."

3. ⟨Write⟩ Find the main idea in the section "The New Immigrants."

_____

_____

_____

_____

_____

_____

📖 **Review: Read for Detail**

⟨Circle⟩ Find one detail that tells where immigrants came from after the law changed in 1965.

Active Reading

Star ▶ Why are politicians paying attention to Latinos?

VOCABULARY BUILDER
Target Word

percent

per•cent (noun)

Rate it: ① ② ③

Meaning

_____

_____

Example

_____

_____

_____

React

Write ▶ Do you think more immigration is good or bad for America? Why?

_____

_____

_____

_____

_____

_____

_____

_____

_____

A Growing Group

Look at the circle graph below about immigrants in our country. Latinos are the biggest immigrant group. They include people from Mexico, Central America, South America, and parts of the Caribbean. In 2000, they made up more than 51 **percent** of all immigrants.

Latino newcomers join other Latinos who have lived in the U.S. for centuries. In 1990, Latinos made up 9 percent of all Americans. By 2000, they had grown to 12.5 percent. They are now the largest minority group.

Politicians pay attention to this trend. They give speeches in Spanish. They join in Latino events. What motivates them? They want Latinos to vote for them!

TEXT FEATURE Reading a Circle Graph

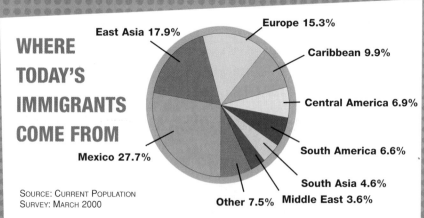

WHERE TODAY'S IMMIGRANTS COME FROM

East Asia 17.9%
Europe 15.3%
Caribbean 9.9%
Central America 6.9%
South America 6.6%
South Asia 4.6%
Middle East 3.6%
Other 7.5%
Mexico 27.7%

Source: Current Population Survey: March 2000

A circle graph shows percentages of a whole.

1. What information does this circle graph show?
- Ⓐ how many people live in the U.S.
- Ⓑ how many immigrants live in the U.S.
- Ⓒ where today's immigrants come from
- Ⓓ what parts of Mexico immigrants come from

2. What color shows the percentage of immigrants from Central America?
- Ⓐ blue
- Ⓒ red
- Ⓑ yellow
- Ⓓ green

3. What percentage of today's immigrants come from:

East Asia? _____   Mexico? _____

Welcome to America?

America was founded on immigration. But are immigrants really welcome today? Yes and no. Some people say that immigration hurts America. They say that immigrants get jobs that American citizens want.

However, others disagree. They say immigrants help America. Many immigrants work for minimum wage. Often, American workers reject those low-income jobs.

Immigrants help in other ways, too. They move to cities that need more workers. They start businesses. They pay taxes. They become citizens. They vote.

Some immigrants are even winning political office. Arnold Schwarzenegger is the governor of California. He was a famous movie star. He's also an immigrant from Austria. "I have gotten all of the opportunities because of America," he says. "I have seen firsthand what it's like to come over here, with empty pockets but full of dreams . . . and to succeed." **END**

| Words to Know! | **minority** a group that is less than half of a whole |

New Americans contribute to the U.S. in many ways.

Main Idea and Details

1. **Write** Find the main idea of "A Growing Group."

_____

_____

_____

_____

_____

_____

2. **Underline** Find two important details in that section.

Skills Check

1. **Write** Find the main idea of "Welcome to America?"

_____

_____

_____

_____

_____

_____

2. **Circle** Find three important details in "Welcome to America?"

TAKE THE WORD CHALLENGE

1 **Fill in.** What percent of your day is spent:

eating? _____

sleeping? _____

watching TV? _____

being in school? _____

2 **Decide.** What do you think the minimum age should be for:

voting in an election? _____

driving? _____

serving in the army? _____

3 **Synonyms**

Synonyms are words that have similar meanings. Examples are *pretty* and *beautiful* or *soldier* and *warrior.*

Match each word to its synonyms below.

communicate	irritable	policy

It's my **policy** to talk to my best friend every night. That's just a **rule** for me!

Synonym

rule, guideline: _____

nervous, jumpy: _____

talk, express: _____

4 **Describe.** What TV commercial has totally influenced you? (meaning you *really, really* want to buy the product)

_____

_____

_____

5 **Pick one.** If you were on a sports team, which statement would motivate you the most to win? Explain why.

☐ "If you don't win, you're all getting kicked off the team!"

☐ "If you win, I'm treating everyone to a pizza party!"

_____

_____

_____

6 **Rate it.** Read these movie theater policies. Write **S** if the policy makes sense. Write **N** if the policy makes no sense.

_____ All beepers and cell phones must be turned off.

_____ No popcorn bags are allowed in the theater.

_____ Movies will be turned off for a 10-minute bathroom break.

7 **Evaluate.** What music do you currently like? List three songs.

1. _____

_____

2. _____

_____

3. _____

_____

8 **Antonyms**

Antonyms are words that have opposite meanings. Examples are *good* and *bad* or *miserable* and *happy*.

Match each word to its antonym below.

isolated	currently	minority

Antonym

formerly: _____

included: _____

majority: _____

Huge

Small

Find the **Word to Know** (p. 10) that is an antonym of the underlined word below.

Freddy Adu finally <u>accepted</u> a deal with a professional team.

Write the antonym here:

_____

9 **Fill in.** Complete these sentences with either income or communicate.

• The boss said, "I'm not raising your _____."

• For many teens, it's easier to _____ with their friends than with their parents.

10 **Fill in.** Complete these sentences with either immigrant or trend.

• A new _____ might not understand American TV shows.

• A new _____ in schools is 7th graders wearing surfer clothes.

Finish

Writing Focus

Expository Paragraph

An **expository paragraph** provides information and explains it.

▶ **Read Melissa's expository paragraph about immigration in her neighborhood in Los Angeles.**

Student Model

The Changing Face of My Neighborhood
by Melissa Chan

My neighborhood in Los Angeles has changed in many ways because of immigration. The most important change has been in my school. Almost 25 percent of the students are newcomers, including my best friend Maria Rios from the Philippines. In addition, many new restaurants have opened. Any day, I can eat food from Ecuador, Malaysia, Mexico, and India. Another important change is the music you hear on the streets. It's mostly Latin, and we all like to salsa dance to it. In conclusion, immigrants have had a big influence on my neighborhood. They've made it a great place to live!

Parts of an Expository Paragraph

▶ **Find these parts of Melissa's expository paragraph.**

1. Underline the sentence that states the **topic**.
2. Check three important **details** that support or explain the topic.
3. Notice the **order** of the details.
4. Circle the **linking words** that connect the ideas.
5. Put a star beside the sentences that **sum up** or restate the topic.

Brainstorm

▶ Read the writing prompt in the middle of the idea web. Then use the boxes to help you brainstorm your ideas.

People

Food

Writing Prompt:
Explain how immigration has changed your neighborhood.

_____

(your neighborhood)

My Own Family

Music

Other Ideas

Plan Your Paragraph

Writing Prompt: Explain how immigration has changed your ~~neighborhood.~~ school.

▶ **Use this chart to plan and organize your paragraph.**

Topic Sentence
• *My neighborhood . . .*
• *Immigration has had a big influence on . . .*
• *In my community, . . .*

Detail 1
• *The most important change . . .*
• *To start with, . . .*
• *First of all, . . .*

Detail 2
• *In addition, . . .*
• *Across town, . . .*
• *On the other hand, . . .*

Detail 3
• *Another important change is . . .*
• *An important difference . . .*
• *A third important change is . . .*

Conclusion
• *In conclusion, . . .*
• *To sum up, . . .*
• *Overall, . . .*

Write Your Paragraph

▶ **Use this writing frame to write a first draft of your paragraph.**

_____
(title)

My neighborhood _____

_____

_____

_____

The most important change _____

_____

_____

In addition, _____

_____

_____

_____

Another important change _____

_____

_____

_____

In conclusion, _____

_____

_____

_____

_____

Revise

▶ **Rate your paragraph. Then have a writing partner rate it.**

Scoring Guide			
weak	okay	good	strong
1	2	3	4

1. Does the first sentence state the **topic**?

| Self | 1 | 2 | 3 | 4 |
| Partner | 1 | 2 | 3 | 4 |

2. Do **details** support or explain the topic?

| Self | 1 | 2 | 3 | 4 |
| Partner | 1 | 2 | 3 | 4 |

3. Are the supporting details in a **logical order**?

| Self | 1 | 2 | 3 | 4 |
| Partner | 1 | 2 | 3 | 4 |

4. Do **linking words** connect the ideas?

| Self | 1 | 2 | 3 | 4 |
| Partner | 1 | 2 | 3 | 4 |

5. Does the ending **sum up** or restate the topic?

| Self | 1 | 2 | 3 | 4 |
| Partner | 1 | 2 | 3 | 4 |

▶ **Now revise your paragraph to make it stronger.**

Grammar IDENTIFYING SENTENCES AND FRAGMENTS

A **sentence** is a group of words that tells a complete idea.

- The subject tells who or what the sentence is about.
- The predicate tells what someone or something does.

Example

Subject	Predicate
Irene's parents	moved to America from Mexico.
My neighbors	are from China and Vietnam.

▶ Identify the underlined part of each sentence below. Write **subject** or **predicate** on the line beside it.

1. My family and I <u>watched a show about immigrants</u>. _____*predicate*_____

2. <u>Three children</u> moved here with their mother. _____

3. Their father <u>came to the U.S. a year later</u>. _____

4. At first, <u>the family</u> had very little money. _____

5. Finally, the father <u>found a job working in a factory</u>. _____

6. <u>The mother and a friend</u> opened their own business. _____

A **sentence fragment** is an incomplete sentence that can't stand by itself. Often, a fragment is missing either a subject or a predicate.

▶ **Rewrite the sentence fragments below as complete sentences.**

7. want their children to grow up in the U.S.

   _____

8. some immigrants from Latin America and Asia

   _____

9. the plane from India

   _____

10. wants to see her grandmother back in Mexico

    _____

 Edit *Take a close look at each of the sentences in your draft on page 25. Do they all express complete ideas? Fix the ones that don't.*

Mechanics USING END PUNCTUATION

Different kinds of sentences use different **end punctuation marks**.

- A statement always ends with a period.
- A question always ends with a question mark.

Example

Statement	Question
I'm from Mexico.	Where are you from?
We are a nation of immigrants.	Were your parents immigrants?

▶ **Find and correct five errors in this paragraph.**

Student Model

My city, New York, has been changed a lot by imigration. See it every day. First of all, some nayborhoods are named after countries, like Chinatown and Little Italy? In addition, you can find a lot of food from other countries here. Another important thing is that I have a lot of friends from other countries. In conclusion, New York has been very influenced by immigration?

Check and Correct

- ☐ Circle two spelling errors and correct them.
- ☐ Underline two end punctuation errors and correct them.
- ☐ Correct one sentence fragment.

Edit ▶ *Look at the sentences in your own draft on page 25. Do they all have the correct end punctuation? Fix the ones that don't.*

Final Draft /Present

▶ **Write a final draft of your paragraph on paper or the computer. Check it again and correct any errors before you present it.**

Translator

New immigrants often need help understanding a new language. Translators can help. Meet Colin Pine, one of the most famous translators in the world. He translates for Yao Ming, the star center for the Houston Rockets. Reporters ask questions, and Colin repeats them to Yao in Chinese. "I want to help Yao learn as much as he can as fast as he can," Colin says.

Name: Colin Pine

Hometown: Houston, Texas

Job: Translator

Duties:
- translates interviews
- translates game plays
- translates conversations

Skills:
- fluency in two or more languages
- ability to communicate clearly

Similar Jobs:
- ESL teacher
- sign-language interpreter
- travel guide

Pay: $35,000 per year

Education: Most translators have a Bachelor's Degree

Colin Pine, at right, translates a question for basketball star Yao Ming.

Ask Yourself

1. **Underline** ▷ Find the section that lists similar jobs. Mark which one interests you most.

2. **Circle** ▷ In the "Skills" list, mark the skill you think you are strongest at.

3. How much do you want this job?
   - ❏ I don't want it.
   - ❏ I might want it.
   - ❏ I really want it.

Using a Daily Schedule

Colin Pine uses a daily schedule to keep track of his time and activities. Fill out the rest of his schedule following the directions below.

Colin Pine's Daily Schedule					
	MON	**TUES**	**WED**	**THURS**	**FRI**
8 A.M.					
9 A.M.					
10 A.M.	*Practice*	*Practice*	*Practice*	*Practice*	*Practice*
11 A.M.					
12 P.M.					
1 P.M.					
2 P.M.					
3 P.M.					
4 P.M.					
5 P.M.					
6 P.M.					
7 P.M.					
8 P.M.					

▶ **Fill in each activity on Colin's schedule above. The first one has been done for you.**

1. Yao Ming has practice from 10 A.M. to 2 P.M. Monday through Friday. Colin must attend each practice.

2. Yao Ming meets with the press for one hour, right after practice on Tuesday. Colin attends to translate.

3. Yao Ming's team has a game that starts at 8 P.M. on Thursday. He has a pregame interview that starts at 7 P.M. Colin must attend both events.

4. Yao Ming is attending a charity dinner on Friday night from 6 P.M. to 8 P.M. Colin Pine must attend and translate.

5. A television program wants to interview Colin Pine about his job and what it's like to be a translator. They want to interview him Monday at 10 A.M., Tuesday at 2 P.M., or Thursday at 8 A.M. Which time works for Colin? Schedule in the interview.

Comprehension

▶ **Fill in the circle next to the correct answer.**

1. Why did Freddy Adu's family move to America?

Ⓐ They had to escape a war.

Ⓑ They wanted to give their kids a better education.

Ⓒ They wanted to get better jobs.

Ⓓ Freddy couldn't play soccer in Ghana, his home country.

2. What word best describes Irene Rodriguez's first year of school in the U.S.?

Ⓐ happy

Ⓑ difficult

Ⓒ successful

Ⓓ boring

> **Here's a tip.**
> Read all the answer choices before answering a question.

3. What is the main idea for this Workshop, "The New Americans"?

Ⓐ Freddy Adu will be a huge star.

Ⓑ Immigration has changed the United States.

Ⓒ People are moving to Latin America.

Ⓓ It's easy to move to the United States.

4. Most new immigrants to America are from _____.

Ⓐ Latin America and Asia

Ⓑ Asia and Africa

Ⓒ Latin America and Europe

Ⓓ Europe

5. Which of the following statements about immigrants is an opinion?

Ⓐ Latinos made up 12.5 percent of the people counted in the 2000 U.S. census.

Ⓑ Immigrants are now moving to cities all over the U.S.

Ⓒ It's easy to make it as an immigrant.

Ⓓ Arnold Schwarzenegger is an immigrant.

Vocabulary

▶ **Fill in the circle next to the correct definition of the underlined word.**

1. It wasn't easy for Irene to be a new <u>immigrant</u>.
   - Ⓐ someone who moves from one country to another country
   - Ⓑ friend
   - Ⓒ a new student in a school
   - Ⓓ pop star

2. Immigrants often <u>influence</u> the communities they live in.
   - Ⓐ change
   - Ⓑ count
   - Ⓒ compare
   - Ⓓ find

3. Today's music <u>trends</u> include an increase in the popularity of Latino music.
   - Ⓐ stars
   - Ⓑ languages
   - Ⓒ patterns of change over time
   - Ⓓ a top-ten list

▶ **Choose the synonyms for the underlined words.**

4. Our class <u>policy</u> is that everyone must <u>communicate</u> respectfully.
   - Ⓐ schedule, dress
   - Ⓑ room, play
   - Ⓒ question, act
   - Ⓓ rule, talk

▶ **Choose the antonym for the underlined word.**

5. My sister spends a <u>minimum</u> of five hours at the mall every weekend.
   - Ⓐ extreme sport
   - Ⓑ maximum
   - Ⓒ least amount
   - Ⓓ fast speed

Short Answer

▶ **Use what you've read in this Workshop to answer the question below. Check your spelling and grammar.**

What challenges do immigrants to the U.S. face?

_____

_____

_____

_____

_____

WORKSHOP 2

NONFICTION

Comprehension Focus
Sequence of Events

READINGS
1 *Struck by Lightning* >> Newspaper Article
2 *A Mountain on Fire* >> Magazine Article
3 *Hurricanes: The Monster Storms* >> Science Text

WHEN DISASTER STRIKES

You can run. You can hide. But you can't escape. No matter where you live, natural disasters can find you. Lightning can strike people in fields and even in buildings. Fires can wipe out huge forests and hundreds of houses. Hurricanes can wreck entire towns!

Have you ever seen the dark side of nature?

VOCABULARY BUILDER

◎ Target Word ▶ Read the Target Words. Rate each one using the scale below.*	Meaning ▶ Read the Target Word meanings. Write in the missing ones.	Example ▶ Finish the Target Word examples below. Write in the missing ones.
destruction de•struc•tion (noun) ① ② ③		Destruction caused by a storm might include . . .
major ma•jor (adjective) ① ② ③	very large or important	
prevent pre•vent (verb) ① ② ③		Things I want to prevent are . . .
recovery re•cov•er•y (noun) ① ② ③	the process of getting back to normal	
severe se•vere (adjective) ① ② ③		 A **severe** storm is headed our way!

*Rating Scale
①= I don't know it at all.
②= I've seen it before.
③= I know it and use it.

The Big Idea

Write What is this article mainly about?

_____

_____

_____

VOCABULARY BUILDER
Target Word

focus

fo•cus (verb)

Rate it: ① ② ③

Meaning

_____

_____

Example

_____

_____

_____

React

Suppose that you saw lightning strike someone. What would you do?

STRUCK BY LIGHTNING
A teen's life changed in a flash!

September 6, 2001— Last month, 16-year-old Justin Norris headed to his after-school job at a fast-food restaurant. It seemed like an ordinary day. But it didn't stay that way for long. Justin was about to get the shock of his life!

Justin Norris survived being struck by lightning.

Justin started work inside the restaurant at the counter. After an hour, he moved to the drive-through window. He took orders from customers through a big menu board. Outside, a severe storm was building. "I heard loud thunder," Justin remembers.

At first, Justin ignored the thunder and **focused** on his work. But the thunder grew louder. Soon, Justin couldn't hear his customers through the speaker. He turned up the volume knob.

Then, a powerful bolt of lightning hit the outdoor menu board. A surge of electricity rushed in. It exceeded 15 million volts! The electricity shot through the board to the knob. Finally, it slammed into Justin's body and knocked him out. He was rushed to the hospital.

At the hospital, Justin had seizures. He couldn't remember names and numbers. The accident had wiped out his memory.

Now Justin is on the road to recovery. Currently, he still has memory loss. But Justin is happy. Why? He knows he's lucky to be alive. **END**

Words to Know! **exceeded** was greater than

Sequence of Events

Sequence is the order in which events happen. To find the sequence of events:

• Try to remember the order in which events take place.

• Look for times, dates, and signal words, such as *first, then, next, after,* and *finally.*

• When you know the order, check it again. Make sure it makes sense.

▶ **Fill in this chart with the sequence of events that led to Justin being struck by lightning.**

At First

Justin ignored the thunder and focused on his work.

Soon

Then

Finally

A MOUNTAIN ON

by Emily Costello

This disaster destroyed a forest and killed firefighters. Find out what happened from those who survived.

The fire on Storm King Mountain in Colorado was one of the worst in U.S. history. It happened over nine hot days in July, 1994.

The Flames Rise

The summer of '94 was hot and dry in Colorado. Rain didn't fall for weeks. The sun baked forests dry. Soon, dozens of fires were burning across the state. Fire crews battled the flames. But the crews were stretched thin.

Then, on July 2nd, flames rose up on Storm King Mountain. It was the start of what would become a monster fire.

At first, firefighters ignored it. They had bigger flames to fight. But, then, the wind changed direction. The fire **increased** in size. Before long, ten acres were up in flames.

FIRE

The Big Blowup

On July 3rd, a team of firefighters headed to Storm King. First, seven of them hiked toward the flames. They cut down trees and dug ditches. At the same time, helicopters dumped water on the flames from above.

But nothing could prevent the fire from spreading. The flames just wouldn't die. It was time to radio for help.

The second day of firefighting began.

About 40 more firefighters joined the crew. At 3:20 P.M., a dry wind swept through the forest. The wind fanned the flames and blew them across a creek. Suddenly, a huge stand of oak trees burst into flames.

Then, the Storm King fire "blew up." A "blow-up" is a sudden jump in a fire's intensity.

"It's going up," one firefighter shouted into his radio. "Everybody get out!" ➡

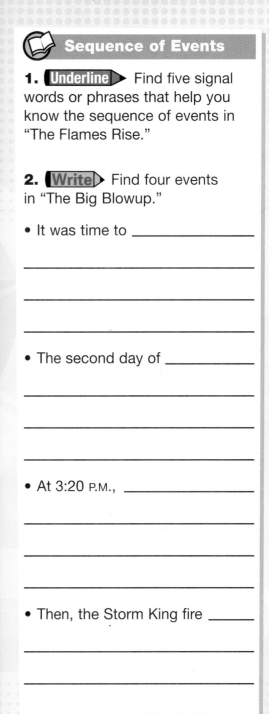

Sequence of Events

1. **Underline** ▶ Find five signal words or phrases that help you know the sequence of events in "The Flames Rise."

2. **Write** ▶ Find four events in "The Big Blowup."

• It was time to _____
_____
_____
_____

• The second day of _____
_____
_____
_____

• At 3:20 P.M., _____
_____
_____
_____

• Then, the Storm King fire _____
_____
_____
_____

Words to Know! **intensity** great strength or extreme degree

VOCABULARY BUILDER
Target Word

degree

de•gree (noun)

Rate it: ① ② ③

Meaning

_____

_____

Example

_____

_____

_____

React

Write What would you be thinking about if you had been stuck in the fire shelter?

_____

_____

_____

_____

_____

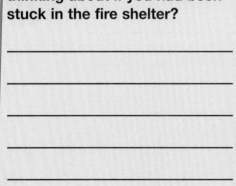

Run For Your Life

The firefighters saw a wall of flames racing toward them. Everyone looked for a way out. "I was running," one firefighter said. "I was scared to death."

Tony Petrilli was the leader of a team. He told his crew to stop running. After that, he ordered his crew to open their fire shelters and crawl inside. The shelters are small metallic tents that keep out flames.

Inside their tents, the firefighters waited. Smoke choked their lungs. Heat burned their skin. Temperatures crept up to over 100 **degrees**. The firefighters knew they might die.

Burnt Out

The fire raged on for two more hours. Then, the wind died down. The flames burned more slowly. At last, the firefighters crawled out.

The Storm King fire raged on until July 11.

"I was running," one firefighter said. "I was scared to death."

They saw destruction everywhere. All that was left of the forest were blackened tree stumps.

The firefighters began to search for their missing friends. After a few hours, they found twelve bodies. The dead had tried to outrun the fire. Days later, two more bodies were found.

By July 11th, the Storm King fire was under control. But for 14 brave firefighters, it was too late. **END**

Words to Know!   **metallic** made of metal

Sequence of Events

▶ Fill in this chart with the events that tell how the firefighters fought and survived the fire from "The Big Blowup" through the end of the article.

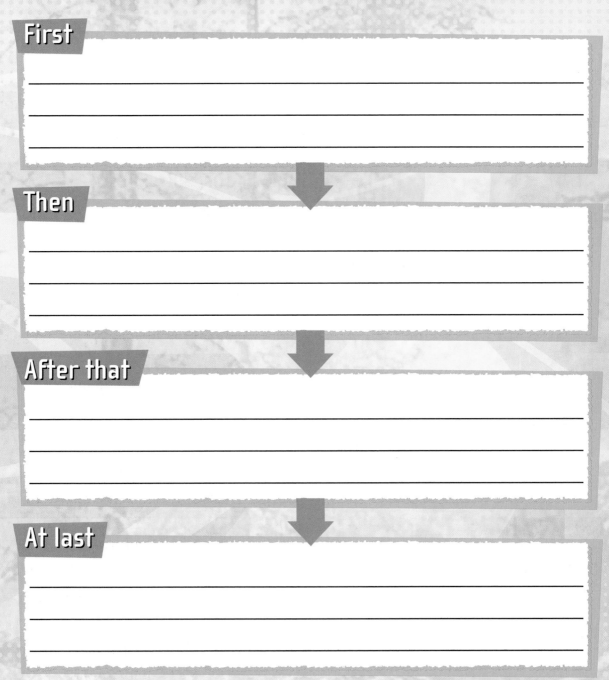

First

_____

_____

_____

Then

_____

_____

_____

After that

_____

_____

_____

At last

_____

_____

_____

The Big Idea

Write What is this article mainly about?

_____

_____

_____

Target Word

abandon

a•ban•don (verb)

Rate it: ① ② ③

Meaning

_____

_____

Example

_____

_____

_____

React

What would *you* say to families that did not want to evacuate?

HURRICANES:
The Monster Storms

How big can a storm be? Six hundred miles across! Hurricanes are the biggest storms on earth. When they hit land, it's a disaster!

Floyd the Destroyer

Hurricane Floyd was one of the most severe hurricanes in recent memory. It was big, wet, tough, and ugly. This major storm landed on U.S. shores in September 1999.

Floyd brought strong winds and heavy rains. The rains caused the most destruction. Floyd dumped 20 inches of water on North Carolina. Floods there exceeded record levels. The hurricane also hit New Jersey and New York. It destroyed homes, farms, and roads. Altogether, Floyd left 68 people dead.

Even before it hit land, scientists knew that Floyd was bad news. Storm trackers flew planes into the hurricane at sea. They measured its strength and size. They warned people to evacuate their homes near the coast.

More than 2.6 million people listened. They **abandoned** their homes. They found shelter in schools and churches. Other people stayed at home—and got the scare of their lives.

Words to Know!   **evacuate** to leave due to an emergency

Above, a satellite photo of Hurricane Floyd as it approached Florida. Below, Kaleatha Vines, a survivor of the storm.

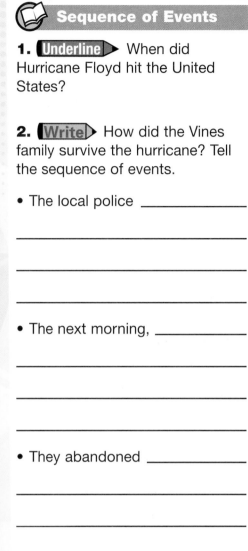

Sequence of Events

1. **Underline** When did Hurricane Floyd hit the United States?

2. **Write** How did the Vines family survive the hurricane? Tell the sequence of events.

• The local police _____

_____

_____

_____

• The next morning, _____

_____

_____

_____

• They abandoned _____

_____

_____

_____

Review: Main Idea and Details

Circle Find the main idea in the section "Refusing to Evacuate."

Refusing to Evacuate

Kaleatha Vines, 14, didn't evacuate before the flood. She and her family lived in Tarboro, North Carolina. They decided to sit out Hurricane Floyd at home. The local police pleaded with the Vineses to evacuate. But nothing could motivate them to leave. "It's not really going to flood," Kaleatha's father insisted.

Her father was wrong. Tarboro was one of the worst hit towns. The next morning, there was knee-deep water in their yard. The family knew they had to leave. They abandoned everything—even their dog!

Driving to the shelter, Kaleatha witnessed the storm's destruction. She saw cars hanging from trees. She saw animals rotting in the streets. The highway was covered with muddy flood waters. Kaleatha was disgusted—and scared. Later, her house had to be rebuilt. Still, she is grateful. Why? She survived. Many other people died. ➡

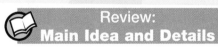

Active Reading

Circle ▶ How fast can a hurricane spin?

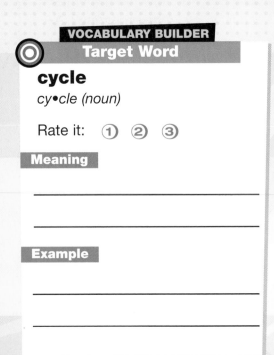

VOCABULARY BUILDER
Target Word

cycle

cy•cle (noun)

Rate it: ①   ②   ③

Meaning

_____

_____

Example

_____

_____

_____

React

Write ▶ If a major storm was coming, who would you want to be there to help you? Why?

_____

_____

_____

_____

_____

How Hurricanes Are Born

A hurricane's life **cycle** begins over the ocean. First, warm, wet air starts to circle over the water. The winds spin slowly. They are spread out over a wide area. The center of the winds is called the eye. If the eye is tiny, tight, and round, a bad storm begins to form.

Then, the warm, moist air rises. The winds begin to spin faster. Soon, the wind and water swirl in a giant cloud above the ocean. When the wind speed reaches 39 miles per hour, a tropical storm is born.

Next, a tropical storm can continue to grow. But it needs warm, wet air rising up off the water. The water temperature must be above 81 degrees Fahrenheit. If the temperature is lower, the storm dies out.

Finally, a tropical storm can turn into a hurricane. How does that happen? When the winds increase to 74 miles per hour, the storm becomes a hurricane. At its fastest, a hurricane can spin over 150 miles per hour!

When Hurricanes Hit

What happens when a hurricane hits land? First, the front wall of the hurricane slams into the coast. It batters trees and houses with high winds. It dumps heavy rains onto the land. Next, the eye of the hurricane passes over. During this time, there is a lull

Words to Know!   **moist** damp

Hurricane Floyd slammed boats into the shore, ruining millions of dollars worth of property.

in the storm. But then, the back wall of the hurricane arrives. The wind picks up strength again.

As a hurricane moves across land, it slowly loses its power. Winds slow down, especially after a storm crosses a mountain. Finally, after about ten days, the hurricane blows itself out. And then, the recovery can begin. (END)

 TEXT FEATURE **Reading a Diagram**

INSIDE A HURRICANE

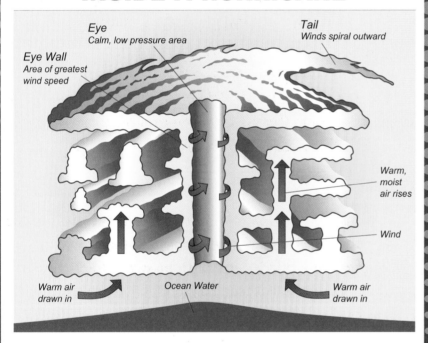

Eye
Calm, low pressure area

Tail
Winds spiral outward

Eye Wall
Area of greatest
wind speed

Warm,
moist
air rises

Wind

Warm air
drawn in

Ocean Water

Warm air
drawn in

A diagram shows you how a process works.

1. What is the very center of the hurricane called?
   Ⓐ the tail   Ⓑ the eye
   Ⓒ the dome   Ⓓ the eye wall

2. From where is warm air drawn into the hurricane?
   Ⓐ the top   Ⓑ the left
   Ⓒ the bottom   Ⓓ the right

3. Where is the fastest part of the hurricane?

_____

 Sequence of Events

1. **Underline** Find the signal words that tell the sequence of events in the section, "How Hurricanes Are Born."

2. **Write** What happens after a tropical storm reaches 74 miles per hour?

_____

_____

_____

_____

_____

_____

_____

_____

Skills Check

1. **Circle** Find the sequence words in the section, "When Hurricanes Hit."

2. **Write** Number these steps in the correct sequence from 1 to 4.
____ The hurricane blows itself out.
____ The front wall of the hurricane hits land.
____ The eye of the hurricane passes over.
____ The hurricane slows down over land.

VOCABULARY

TAKE THE WORD CHALLENGE

Start

1 **Rate.** Which causes the most severe destruction in your state? Which causes the least?

1 = least severe
4 = most severe

_____ floods

_____ fires

_____ tornadoes

_____ earthquakes

- - - - - - - -

2 **Use this scale.** Can you prevent:

	yes	maybe	never
a hurricane	☐	☐	☐
a pimple	☐	☐	☐
a fistfight	☐	☐	☐
a cold	☐	☐	☐

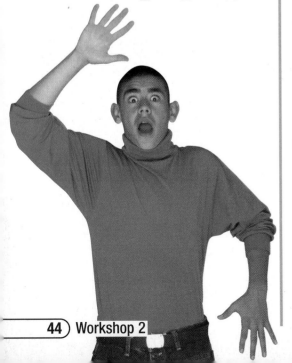

3 **Prefixes**

A **prefix** is a letter or a group of letters added to the beginning of a word. A prefix changes the meaning of a word. The prefix *re-* means "again." So, *re*count means "to count again." *Re*read means "to read again."

Define. All of these words use the prefix *re-*. Guess what the words mean, using your knowledge of the prefix.

I love this song! I've already **replayed** it 100 times.

☐ recycle   *to cycle again* _____

☐ revisit   _____

☐ reuse   _____

☐ redo   _____

4 **Check two.** Which two weather forecasts sound the worst to you?

☐ "Winds tomorrow will exceed 80 mph!"

☐ "Tomorrow's temperature will exceed 100 degrees!"

☐ "The snowfall will exceed four inches tomorrow!"

☐ "The weather for the parade exceeds our highest hopes!"

- - - - - - - -

5 **List.** Look at the list of events below. Write a personal example for each. Be ready to explain what made each major for you.

A major birthday: _____

A major embarrassment: _____

A major scare: _____

8 Suffixes

A **suffix** is a letter or group of letters added to the end of a word. A suffix changes the meaning or part of speech of a word. The suffix *-ion* turns a verb into a noun. *Evacuate* is a verb. *Evacuation* is a noun.

Fill in. Turn these verbs into nouns by adding the suffix *-ion*.

prevent: _____

complicate: _____

construct: _____

educate: _____

evacuate + ion = evacuation

6 Analyze. Who causes accidents on the road? Put *A* for agree and *D* for disagree.

_____ Mothers increase the risk of accidents.

_____ Teen drivers increase the risk of accidents.

_____ Sleepy drivers increase the risk of accidents.

_____ Teachers increase the risk of accidents.

7 Fill in. If I had to evacuate my home . . .

I might abandon:

_____

I would definitely abandon:

_____

I would never abandon:

_____

9 Evaluate. The best way to eat a worm is to chew slowly and focus on how it tastes.

True   False

Why? _____

_____

_____

_____

10 Rate. How long would it take you to recover from . . .

a scary movie:

_____

a fight with a friend:

_____

a broken leg:

_____

Finish

When Disaster Strikes **45**

Writing Focus
Narrative Paragraph

A **narrative paragraph** tells a story about an event.

▶ **Read James's narrative paragraph about a disaster in his town.**

Student Model

The Tornado
by James Washington

When I was 8, a major tornado hit my hometown of Cincinnati, Ohio. At first, the sky turned yellow-gray, and hail began to fall. The hail was the size of softballs. Then the rain started to pound on our roof. The wind blew hard enough to make the trees bend. After that, my mother took us into the basement. We stayed there and listened to the radio. The reporter said that a severe storm was passing over our area. Later, he said the storm had finally passed, and it was safe to come out. The next day, we saw the destruction that the tornado had caused. We knew then how lucky we had been!

Parts of a Narrative Paragraph
▶ **Find these parts of James's narrative paragraph.**

1. Underline the sentence that tells about the **event**.
2. Check three **details** about the event.
3. Number these details in the **time order** they happened.
4. Circle the **linking words** that connect the details.
5. Put a star before the sentences that **sum up** the event and tell the writer's feelings about it.

Brainstorm

▶ Read the writing prompt in the middle of the idea web. Then, use the boxes to help you brainstorm your ideas.

Coldest Weather

Hottest Weather

Writing Prompt:
Tell about a time when you experienced severe weather.

Wettest Weather

Wildest Weather

Plan Your Paragraph

Writing Prompt: Tell about a time when you experienced severe weather.

▶ Use this chart to plan and organize your paragraph.

Word Choices

_____

_____

_____

_____

_____

Event
• *When I was . . .*
• *The worst weather I ever saw was . . .*
• *The weather changed so suddenly . . .*

Detail 1
• *At first, . . .*
• *The first thing I noticed . . .*
• *In the beginning, . . .*

Detail 2
• *Then, . . .*
• *The next thing I knew, . . .*
• *Before long, . . .*

Detail 3
• *After that, . . .*
• *Suddenly, . . .*
• *At that moment, . . .*

Ending
• *Finally, . . .*
• *In the end, . . .*
• *Once it was over, . . .*

Write Your Paragraph

▶ Use this writing frame to write a first draft of your paragraph.

_____
(title)

When I was _____

_____

_____

_____

At first, _____

_____

_____

_____

Then, _____

_____

_____

_____

After that, _____

_____

_____

_____

Finally, _____

_____

_____

_____

_____

Revise

▶ Rate your paragraph. Then have a writing partner rate it.

Scoring Guide			
weak	okay	good	strong
1	2	3	4

1. Does the beginning clearly state the **event**?

Self   1   2   3   4

Partner   1   2   3   4

2. Are there **details** that tell about the event?

Self   1   2   3   4

Partner   1   2   3   4

3. Are the details arranged in the **time order** they happened?

Self   1   2   3   4

Partner   1   2   3   4

4. Do **linking words** connect the details?

Self   1   2   3   4

Partner   1   2   3   4

5. Does the ending **sum up** the event and tell the writer's feelings about it?

Self   1   2   3   4

Partner   1   2   3   4

▶ Now revise your paragraph to make it stronger.

Grammar CORRECTING SENTENCE FRAGMENTS

A **sentence fragment** is an incomplete sentence. Often, sentence fragments are missing a subject or a verb. To fix some fragments, add a subject or verb to make a complete sentence.

Example

Sentence Fragment	Complete Sentence
A tornado our town today. [missing verb] Brought the tree down. [missing subject]	A tornado struck our town today. A storm brought the tree down.

▶ **Write whether each fragment below is missing a subject or a verb.**

1. The wind outside against the trees. _____verb_____

2. Beat my window and kept me awake all night. _____

3. Some trees from the park on Main Street. _____

4. Finally, after the wind died down, went outside. _____

5. The next day, only a shower. _____

To correct some **sentence fragments**, you can connect the fragment to a complete sentence by adding a comma and any missing words.

Example

Sentence and Fragment	Complete Sentence
A tornado struck our town today. Touched down in Texas.	A tornado struck our town today, and then it touched down in Texas.

▶ **Rewrite each sentence and fragment as one complete sentence.**

6. We studied storms in class. Including tornadoes.

_____

7. Storms are fun to study. Not to experience yourself.

_____

8. Our teacher led an experiment. Then a quiz.

_____

9. We all expected a test. But not until Friday.

_____

 Take a close look at each of the sentences in your draft on page 49. Do they all express complete thoughts? Fix the ones that don't.

Mechanics USING CAPITALS

Some words begin with a **capital letter**.

- The first word in a sentence begins with a capital letter.
- A proper noun begins with a capital letter.

Example

Correct	Incorrect
Lightning struck the building.	lightning struck the building.
The storm flooded Emily's home.	The storm flooded emily's home.

▶ **Find and correct five errors in this paragraph.**

Student Model

When my brother ralph was a baby, our house was flooded. That spring, it rained every day. Soon, the river began to rise. one day, water covered the road. A boat carried us to saftey, but the river kept rising. Finally, we went back to our house. Mud on the walls two feet high. For weeks, the house smelled bad. The flood caused lots of destrucktion!

Check and Correct

- ☐ Circle two spelling errors and correct them.
- ☐ Underline two capitalization errors and correct them.
- ☐ Correct one sentence fragment.

Edit Look at the sentences in your own draft on page 49. Do they all use capitals correctly? Fix the ones that don't.

Final Draft/Present

▶ **Write a final draft of your paragraph on paper or the computer. Check it again and correct any errors before you present it.**

EMT-Paramedic

Rodrigo Castillo saves lives for a living. He's an EMT-Paramedic, the most advanced type of emergency medical technician. In his ambulance, Castillo is the first to show up after someone calls 911 during a medical emergency. "Every day is different," he says. "You arrive at work and don't know what the day will bring."

Name: Rodrigo Castillo, Jr.

Hometown: Santa Maria, California

Job: EMT-Paramedic

Duties:
- drives to emergency calls
- treats people in medical emergencies
- monitors patients during the trip to the hospital

Skills:
- ability to stay calm during high-stress, life-and-death situations
- ability to follow strict rules and guidelines about medical care
- strength to lift people onto stretchers

Similar Jobs:
- Emergency Medical Technician
- ER Nurse

Pay: $52,000 to $60,000 per year

Above, Rodrigo stands in front of the van he drives to emergencies. Below, he demonstrates the lifesaving care he gives to patients inside the van.

Education: attend paramedic school, do internship, and pass state exam

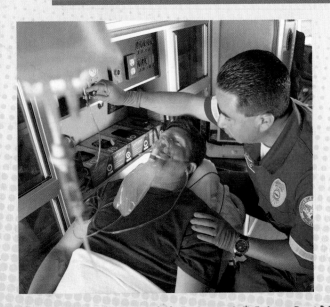

Ask Yourself

1. **Underline** How much money does an EMT-Paramedic make?

2. **Circle** Which duty do you think you'd be best at if you were a paramedic?

3. How much do you want this job?

   ❑ I don't want it.

   ❑ I might want it.

   ❑ I really want it.

Following CPR Instructions

A paramedic like Rodrigo Castillo has to follow medical instructions exactly. People's lives depend on it! Giving CPR to ill people is part of his job. CPR stands for cardiopulmonary resuscitation. That means assisting someone whose heart and lungs have stopped functioning on their own. CPR is best done by someone with training. This chart can give you an idea of how it's done for an adult victim.

► **Fill in the circle next to each correct answer.**

1. If you find someone who is no longer breathing, what should you do first?

Ⓐ Look for ID.

Ⓑ Call 911.

Ⓒ Give two breaths.

Ⓓ Check if the person is breathing.

2. When should the chin be lifted?

Ⓐ after you give up

Ⓑ before calling 911

Ⓒ when the chest is pushed down

Ⓓ when checking breathing

Step 1: Call 911

Step 2: Tilt head, lift chin, check breathing

Step 3: Give two breaths

Step 4: Position hands in the center of chest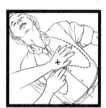

Step 5: Firmly push down two inches on the chest 15 times

Continue with two breaths and 15 pumps until help arrives.

3. In Step 4, where should the hands be placed?

Ⓐ under the throat

Ⓑ at the center of the chest

Ⓒ over each lung

Ⓓ at the diaphragm

4. In Step 5, how many times should you push down on the chest?

Ⓐ 15 times

Ⓑ until help arrives

Ⓒ until someone calls 911

Ⓓ can't tell

5. When should you give someone CPR?

Ⓐ if the person has stopped talking

Ⓑ if the person's heart and lungs have stopped functioning on their own

Ⓒ if the person is very upset and hurt

Ⓓ if the person is burned from a fire

Comprehension

▶ **Fill in the circle next to the correct answer.**

1. Lightning struck Justin Norris when he was _____.
   - Ⓐ hiking in a forest
   - Ⓑ on his way to school in a car
   - Ⓒ working at a fast-food restaurant
   - Ⓓ at home asleep

2. During the Storm King fire, when did firefighters crawl into their shelters?
   - Ⓐ right after the fire started
   - Ⓑ when they couldn't outrun the fire
   - Ⓒ when they arrived at Storm King Mountain
   - Ⓓ when they finished fighting the fire

> **Here's a tip.**
> For fill-in-the-blank questions, substitute each answer for the blank in the sentence. Then pick the best one.

3. What kind of destruction does a hurricane cause?
   - Ⓐ It shakes the ground under houses and destroys them.
   - Ⓑ It starts fires and destroys forests.
   - Ⓒ It strikes people at their jobs and knocks them unconscious.
   - Ⓓ It blows houses over and causes floods.

4. When a hurricane is coming, people should _____.
   - Ⓐ stay at home
   - Ⓑ evacuate their homes
   - Ⓒ go to a boat to stay safe
   - Ⓓ get into small, heat-resistant shelters

5. Where is a hurricane most likely to happen?
   - Ⓐ on tall mountains
   - Ⓑ near an ocean
   - Ⓒ in forests
   - Ⓓ at the earth's poles

Vocabulary

▶ **Fill in the circle next to the correct definition of the underlined word.**

1. Hurricane Floyd caused <u>major</u> flooding in many areas of the South.
   - Ⓐ very small or unimportant
   - Ⓑ frightening
   - Ⓒ very large or important
   - Ⓓ deep and cold

2. After being struck by lightning, Justin had a long <u>recovery</u> period.
   - Ⓐ the process of getting better
   - Ⓑ hospitalized
   - Ⓒ uncomfortable
   - Ⓓ disturbing

3. If you hear a <u>severe</u> storm warning on the news, you wait for more information.
   - Ⓐ very fun and amusing
   - Ⓑ very wet and windy
   - Ⓒ very scary or exciting
   - Ⓓ very bad or serious

▶ **What does the prefix in the underlined word mean?**

4. If you <u>recycle</u> newspapers, fewer trees have to be cut down for paper.
   - Ⓐ not
   - Ⓑ again
   - Ⓒ extra
   - Ⓓ back

▶ **Fill in the circle next to the words that best complete the sentence.**

5. Educating people about fire _____ can stop the _____ of forests.
   - Ⓐ prevent, destroy
   - Ⓑ prevention, destruction
   - Ⓒ prevented, destroyed
   - Ⓓ preventer, destroyer

Short Answer

▶ **Use what you've read in this Workshop to answer the question below. Check your spelling and grammar.**

Which natural disaster do you think is the worst?

_____

_____

_____

_____

_____

WORKSHOP 3

LITERATURE

Comprehension Focus
Story Elements

READINGS

1 *Louisa, Please Come Home* >> Short Story
2 *I'm Nobody! Who are you?* >> Poetry
3 *A Whole New Look* >> Poetry

Identity Crisis

Have you ever felt like people don't really know you? Shirley Jackson asks this question in her story, "Louisa, Please Come Home." Jackson is famous for her creepy stories with weird twist endings.

In this story, Louisa decides to run away from home. Find out what happens when she tries to come back.

VOCABULARY BUILDER

⊙ Target Word ▶ Read the Target Words. Rate each one using the scale below.*	**Meaning** ▶ Read the Target Word meanings. Write in the missing ones.	**Example** ▶ Finish the Target Word examples below. Write in the missing ones.
deceive de•ceive (verb) ① ② ③		I would never deceive . . .
identity i•den•ti•ty (noun) ① ② ③	who a person is	
impostor im•pos•tor (noun) ① ② ③		An example of an impostor is . . .
recognize rec•og•nize (verb) ① ② ③	to see someone and know who the person is	
unique u•nique (adjective) ① ② ③		I dyed my hair so I would look **unique**.

*Rating Scale
①= I don't know it at all.
②= I've seen it before.
③= I know it and use it.

Comprehension Focus
Story Elements

A **short story** like "Louisa, Please Come Home" is a brief piece of fiction. To understand a short story, look for four elements:

1. **Setting** is where and when the story takes place. This story takes place in a city during the 1950s.

2. **Characters** are the people in the story.

Louisa Tether,
a 19-year-old girl

Mr. and Mrs. Tether and Carol,
Louisa's family

Mrs. Peacock,
owner of a
rooming house

Paul, Louisa's
neighbor

3. **Plot** is the sequence of events in a story. The plot contains a problem that the main character needs to solve. In "Louisa, Please Come Home," the main character runs away from home. But she faces a big problem when she decides to return.

4. **Theme** is the message about life that the author wants to express.

▶ **Turn the page to begin reading Louisa's story.**

Louisa, Please Come Home

▶ Fill in this chart as you reread the story.

	Part 1 (pp. 60–61)	Part 2 (pp. 62–67)	Part 3 (pp. 68–69)
Setting	Time: _June 20, in the 1950s_ Place: _a city called Chandler_	Time: Place:	Time: Place:
Character	Who is the main character? Describe him/her:	How does the character change?	What is the character like now?
Plot Events	What happens at the beginning of the story?	What happens in the middle of the story?	How does the story end?
Theme	Author's message:		

Active Reading

Write When Louisa leaves home, what is everybody getting ready for?

_____

_____

_____

VOCABULARY BUILDER
Target Word

error

er•ror (noun)

Rate it: ③

Meaning

_____

_____

Example

_____

_____

_____

 React

Why might someone run away from home?

Louisa, Please Come Home

adapted from the story by **Shirley Jackson**

I listened to my mother's trembling voice over the radio. "Louisa," she said, "please come home. It's been three years since we saw you. We all miss you, and we want you back again. Louisa, please come home."

Once a year I heard that announcement on the anniversary of the day I ran away. I also read the newspaper stories about myself. "Louisa Tether disappeared one year ago." Or two years, or three. I used to wait for June 20 as if it were my birthday.

I was residing in Chandler. It was a big enough city for me to hide in. It was also near my old home, so the papers always made a big fuss about my anniversary.

Words to Know!	**residing** living in a particular place

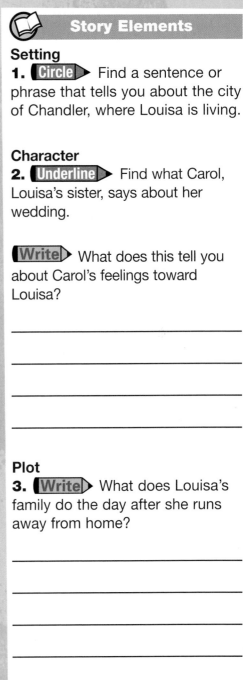

Story Elements

Setting
1. **Circle** Find a sentence or phrase that tells you about the city of Chandler, where Louisa is living.

Character
2. **Underline** Find what Carol, Louisa's sister, says about her wedding.

Write What does this tell you about Carol's feelings toward Louisa?

_____

_____

_____

_____

Plot
3. **Write** What does Louisa's family do the day after she runs away from home?

_____

_____

_____

_____

Now go to page 59. Add details to Part 1 of the chart.

I didn't decide to leave home on the spur of the moment. I had been planning it for a long time. I knew that everything had to go just right because if I made any **errors**, I would have looked like a ridiculous fool. My sister Carol would never have let me forget that.

I admit I planned my departure for the day before Carol's wedding. The newspapers reported that my family had the wedding anyway. Carol told a reporter that her sister Louisa would have wanted it that way.

"She would never have wanted to spoil my wedding," Carol explained. But secretly, she knew that was exactly what I'd wanted.

Anyway, on that day, everyone was hurrying around the house, making preparations for the wedding. I just walked out the door and started my new life. →

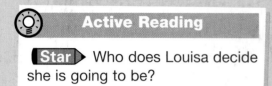

Active Reading

Star Who does Louisa decide she is going to be?

VOCABULARY BUILDER
Target Word

genuinely

gen•u•ine•ly (adverb)

Rate it: ① ② ③

Meaning

truly or sincerely

Example

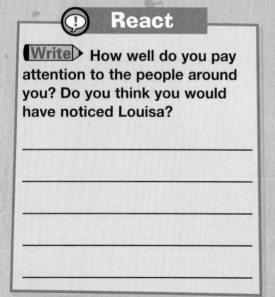

React

Write How well do you pay attention to the people around you? Do you think you would have noticed Louisa?

There was only one bad minute when Paul saw me. Paul lived next door to us, and Carol hates him more than she hates me. My mother can't stand him, either.

Of course, Paul didn't know I was running away. I told him the exact same story I had told my parents. I was going downtown to get away from all the confusion and excitement. Paul wanted to come with me, but I ran for the bus and left him standing there.

I rode the bus downtown and then walked to the railroad station. I purchased a round-trip ticket to Crain to make them think I was planning to return. That way they wouldn't start looking for me too quickly.

I knew they'd think I would stay in Crain. It was the biggest city the train went to. But my plan was to stay there for only part of one day.

To change my appearance, I bought a tan raincoat in a department store in Crain. I had left home wearing a conspicuous new jacket. I just left the jacket on a counter in the store. Someone probably bought it.

I was pretty confident about one thing: There must be thousands of 19-year-old girls, fair-haired, five feet four inches tall, weighing 126 pounds. And a lot of them would be wearing shapeless tan raincoats. I wouldn't be unique, and nobody would detect me.

It's funny how no one pays any attention to you. Hundreds of people saw me that day, but no one really *saw* me.

I took a train to Chandler, which is the place where I'd been heading all along. I slept on the train.

When I got there, I bought a suitcase, stockings, and a little clock. I put the other items in the suitcase. Then I was ready to get settled in Chandler. Nothing is hard to do unless you get upset or excited about it.

Words to Know! **conspicuous** very easy to notice

I decided what my new identity would be. I was a 19-year-old girl named Lois Taylor who had a nice family upstate. I had saved enough money to come live in Chandler. When the summer ended, I would go to business school. I would need a job to pay for it.

I stopped in a drugstore for breakfast and a paper. I read the ads for furnished rooms. Everything about me appeared so normal—suitcase, raincoat, rooms for rent. When I asked the clerk at the drugstore how to get to Primrose Street, he never even glanced at me.

I walked into Mrs. Peacock's house on Primrose Street, and right away, I knew this was the perfect place. My room was nice, and Mrs. Peacock and I **genuinely** liked each other.

She was pleased that my mother wanted me to find a clean room in a good neighborhood. And she was even more pleased that I wanted to save money so I could send some home every week.

→

Setting

1. Circle What two cities does Louisa go to?

Write In which city does she stay?

_____

Character

2. Write How would you describe Louisa's personality?

calm and matter-of-fact

_____

_____

Plot

3. Write What important events happen in this part of the story?

Sees Paul
Runs away
Moves to Chandler
Finds a place to live
Finds a job
Makes up a new identity.

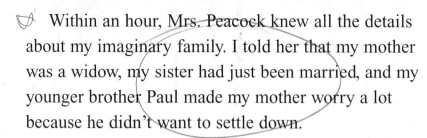

Within an hour, Mrs. Peacock knew all the details about my imaginary family. I told her that my mother was a widow, my sister had just been married, and my younger brother Paul made my mother worry a lot because he didn't want to settle down.

Mrs. Peacock was eager to take care of me. She told me about a job in a stationery store. So there I was. I had been away from home for 24 hours, and already I was a whole new person. I was Lois Taylor. I lived on Primrose Street and worked at the stationery store.

In the mornings, Mrs. Peacock and I would read the newspapers during breakfast. She'd ask my opinion about the girl who disappeared over in Rockville. I'd say she must be insane to leave a nice home like that.

Once I picked up the newspaper and looked intently at the picture. "Do you think she looks like me?" I asked Mrs. Peacock.

"No," Mrs. Peacock **responded**. "Her hair is longer, and her face is fatter than yours."

"I think she kind of resembles me," I said.

My picture appeared in the Chandler papers a lot, but no one ever looked at me twice. I went to work, I shopped in the stores, and I went to the movies and the beach with Mrs. Peacock. Still, no one recognized me. I had done a perfect job of changing my identity.

One morning, Mrs. Peacock was reading about my disappearance. "They're saying now that she was kidnapped," she said.

"I feel kind of sorry for her," I said.

"You can never tell," she said. "Maybe she went willingly with the kidnapper."

On the anniversary of my running away, I bought a new hat. When I got home, Mrs. Peacock was listening to the radio. I heard my mother's familiar voice.

"Louisa," she said, "please come home."

"That poor woman," Mrs. Peacock said. "Imagine how she must feel. She hasn't given up hope of finding her little girl alive some day."

I decided not to go to business school after all, since the stationery store was expanding, and I would probably be a manager soon. Mrs. Peacock and I agreed it would be foolish to give up such a secure job.

By this time, I had some savings in the bank. I was adjusting to my new life. I never had a thought about returning home. It was just plain bad luck that I had an encounter with Paul. ➡

Words to Know!	**expanding** getting bigger

Local News
Rockville Girl Still Missing

Story Elements

Setting
1. **Write** When do Louisa and Mrs. Peacock read the newspaper together?

_____

_____

Character
2. **Underline** Find two sentences or phrases that tell how Louisa feels about her new life.

Plot
3. **Write** What happens on Louisa's anniversary of running away?

_____

_____

_____

_____

_____

Review: Read for Detail

Write What did Louisa buy for herself on the anniversary of the day she ran away?

_____

Literature

Active Reading

Star ▷ What threat does Paul make to Louisa?

⊚ **Target Word**

precisely

pre•cise•ly *(adverb)*

Rate it:

Meaning

_____

_____

Example

_____

_____

_____

_____

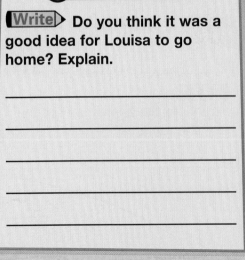

React

Write ▷ Do you think it was a good idea for Louisa to go home? Explain.

_____

_____

_____

_____

_____

I didn't stop to think when I recognized him on the street. I automatically yelled, "Paul!"

He turned around and stared at me with a shocked expression on his face. Then he said, "Is it possible?"

He said I had to go back. If I didn't, he threatened to tell my parents where I was. He told me there was still a reward for anyone who found me, and assured me that I could run away again after he got the reward.

Maybe I really wanted to go home; maybe that's why I yelled his name out on the street. Anyway, I decided to go with him.

I told Mrs. Peacock that I was leaving to visit my family upstate. I thought that was funny. Paul sent a telegram to my mother and father.

When we arrived in Rockville, we took a taxi to my house. I began to get nervous as I looked out the window. I would have sworn that I hadn't thought about Rockville for three years, but I remembered it all **precisely**, as if I had never been away.

The taxi turned onto my street. When I saw the house, I almost cried. "Everything looks just the same," I said. "I caught the bus right there on the corner."

"If I had managed to stop you that day," Paul said, "you would probably never have tried again."

As we walked up the driveway, I wondered if my family was watching from the window, and if I'd have to ring the doorbell. I'd never had to ring it before.

I was still wondering when Carol opened the door. "Carol!" I said. I was genuinely glad to see her.

Carol looked at me hard, then she stepped back and I saw my mother and father. I was going to run to them, but I held myself back. I wasn't sure if they were angry with me, or hurt, or happy that I was back.

I wasn't sure of what to say, so I just stood there and said, "Mother?" kind of uncertainly.

She put her hands on my shoulders, and then looked at my face for a long time. There were tears running down her cheeks, and she looked old and sad.

Then she turned to Paul and said, "Oh Paul, how could you do this to me again?" ➡

Words to Know! | **assured** promised

Setting

1. Write How does the setting in this part of the story change?

_____

_____

_____

_____

Character

2. Underline Find how Louisa feels about her sister when she sees her.

Plot

3. Write What problem does Louisa have when she sees her family?

_____

_____

_____

_____

_____

Now go to page 59. Add details to Part 2 of the chart.

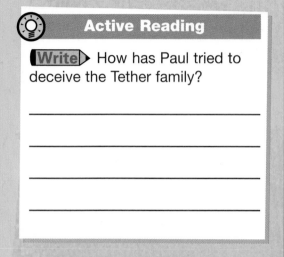

Active Reading

Write How has Paul tried to deceive the Tether family?

_____

_____

_____

_____

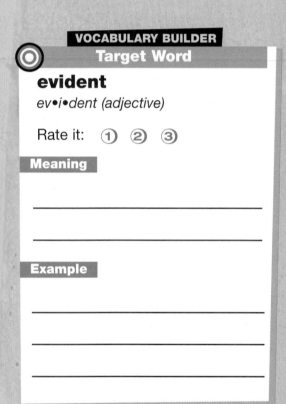

VOCABULARY BUILDER
Target Word

evident

ev•i•dent *(adjective)*

Rate it: ① ② ③

Meaning

_____

_____

Example

_____

_____

_____

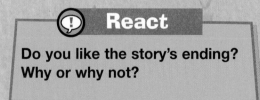

React

Do you like the story's ending? Why or why not?

Paul looked frightened. "Mrs. Tether—"

My mother asked me, "What is your name, dear?"

"Louisa Tether," I said stupidly.

"No, dear," she said very gently. "Your real name."

Now I felt like crying. "Louisa Tether," I said. "That's my name."

"Why don't you people leave us alone?" Carol screamed. "We've spent years trying to find my sister. And people like you just try to cheat us out of the reward money—and we get hurt and heartbroken all over again."

"Carol," my father said, "you're frightening the poor child. Young lady," he said to me, "I don't think you realize the cruelty of what you are doing. You look like a nice girl. Try to imagine how your own mother would feel if someone did this to her."

I tried to imagine my own mother. I looked straight at her.

My father said, "I'm sure this young man didn't tell you he's taken advantage of us before. He's tried to deceive us twice when he's brought us girls who pretended to be our Louisa. The first time we were fooled for several days. The girl *looked* like our Louisa, and she *acted* like our Louisa. She even knew about personal family things that only Louisa—or Paul—could know. But she was not our daughter. She was an impostor. And my wife suffers more each time her hopes are raised."

He put one arm around my mother and the other around Carol. They all stood there staring at me.

Paul started to argue with them. I suddenly realized that all I wanted was to stay here, but it was **evident** that I couldn't. They had made up their minds that I wasn't Louisa.

"Paul," I said, "can't you see that you're only making Mr. Tether angry?"

"Correct, young lady," my father said.

"Paul," I said, "these people don't want us here." Paul was about to argue again, but instead, he turned and stomped off toward the door.

I turned to follow him. My father—I mean Mr. Tether—came up behind me and took my hand. "My daughter was younger than you," he said in a gentle tone. "But I'm certain you have a family somewhere. Go back to the people who love you."

That meant Mrs. Peacock, I guess.

"To make sure you get there," my father said, "I want you to take this." He put a folded bill in my hand. "I hope someone will do as much for our Louisa."

"Good-bye, my dear," my mother said, and reached up and patted my cheek. "Good luck to you."

"I hope your daughter comes back some day," I told them. "Good-bye."

The bill was a twenty, and I gave it to Paul. He'd gone to a lot of trouble, and I still had my job at the stationery store.

My mother still talks to me on the radio, once a year, on the anniversary of the day I ran away.

"Louisa," she says, "please come home. We all want our dear girl back, and we need you and miss you so much. Your mother and father love you and will never forget you. Louisa, please come home." END

Words to Know! **tone** a way of speaking that shows a certain feeling

Story Elements

Setting
1. **Write** Where is Louisa living at the end of the story?

_____

_____

Character
2. **Underline** What are Louisa's last words to her family?

Theme
3. **Check** Which do you think is the author's main message?
- ☐ Never run away from home.
- ☐ Your family may not know the person you really are.
- ☐ You only appreciate something after you've lost it.

Now go to page 59. Complete Part 3 of the chart and the theme.

Skills Check

1. **Write** What new problem does Louisa have?

_____

_____

_____

2. **Write** How have Louisa's feelings about her family changed?

_____

_____

_____

Active Reading

Write What happens when the speaker of the second poem goes to school on Friday?

_____

_____

_____

_____

_____

React

Write Which poem do you like the most? Why?

_____

_____

_____

_____

_____

_____

I'm Nobody! Who are you?

by Emily Dickinson

I'm Nobody! Who are you?
Are you—Nobody—too?
Then there's a pair of us!
Don't tell! they'd advertise—
    you know!

How dreary—to be—Somebody!
How public—like a Frog—
To tell one's name—
    the livelong June—
To an admiring Bog!

A Whole New Look

by Angela Shelf Medearis

I got my braces taken off on Tuesday.
I got my hair cut and a curly perm on Wednesday.
I got contacts on Thursday.
Friday when I went to school
no one knew who I was.

Literary Elements: Rhyme and Repetition

Rhyme is two or more words that have ending syllables with the same sound.

Circle ▶ Find the words that rhyme in "I'm Nobody! Who are you?"

Repetition is words, phrases, or sentences that are used over and over again.

Underline ▶ Find the phrases that repeat in "A Whole New Look."

Literary Elements: Theme

Theme is the message about life that the author wants to express.

Write ▶ How do these poems remind you of "Louisa, Please Come Home"?

_____
_____
_____
_____
_____
_____

TAKE THE WORD CHALLENGE

Start

1 **Think about it.** If you won a million dollars, how would you respond? Write *yes, no,* or *maybe* beside each choice.

_____ I'd put all the money in the bank.

_____ I'd have a huge party.

_____ I'd share it with my family.

2 **Decide.** What part of your identity is most unique?

❑ your laugh

❑ your temper

❑ your handwriting

❑ your clothes

3 **Verb Endings**

A **verb ending** can be added to a verb to show when an action takes place. To show that an action happened in the past, you can often add *-ed*. To show that an action happens in the present, you can often add *-ing*. If a verb ends with an *e*, it is usually dropped before adding *-ed* or *-ing*.

> Sometimes, I *exercise*.
> Yesterday, I *exercised*.
> Right now, I am *exercising*.

Add the verb. Use the correct verb ending.

1. Yesterday, she _____ the CD I gave her. (play)

2. Today, we _____ to get tickets to the concert. (want)

3. They are _____ us to the box office right now. (drive)

I **listen** to a ton of music! Yesterday, I **listened** to eight CDs. Really!

4 **Fill in.** Complete these sentences with genuinely or error.

In today's soccer game, my

biggest _____ was

scoring a point for the other

team. I was _____

embarrassed!

5 **Check it.** Which statements might people who were trying to deceive you say?

❑ "Let's do some yard work. Pulling weeds will be lots of fun."

❑ "If you forward this email, you'll have good luck."

❑ "A bee is about to sting you!"

❑ "Just tell me. I promise I'll keep it a secret."

6 Choose one. Who do you think is the biggest impostor?

- ☐ a singer who lip-syncs
- ☐ an actor in a play
- ☐ a person who imitates a celebrity

7 Tell. Some things need to be done precisely. Some things don't. Write *precisely* or *not precisely* next to each action.

brain surgery_____

watering the lawn_____

counting change_____

8 Word Families

A **word family** is a group of words that share the same base word and have related meanings, such as *receive* and *receipt*. *Receive* means to be given something. A *receipt* is a piece of paper that shows that you have received something.

Which sentences use words that come from the same word family as *identity*?

- ☐ How will we identify the thief?
- ☐ I can't let you in without identification.
- ☐ My teeth fell out. I need dentures.

I'm so thankful to **receive** this gift!

I hope you like it. But if you don't, I still have the **receipt**.

9 Check. Which of these people have voices you would recognize over the phone?

- ☐ your mother
- ☐ a local newspaper reporter
- ☐ your favorite movie star
- ☐ the President of the United States
- ☐ your first-grade teacher

10 Think. Use clues. Check the answer.

She yawned a lot and fell asleep in class.

It was really evident that:
- ☐ she was tired.
- ☐ she was lazy.

It was also evident that:
- ☐ she needed a laugh.
- ☐ she needed more sleep.

Finish

Writing Focus

Literature Response

In a literature response, a reader relates a piece of literature to his or her life.

▶ **Read Maureen's literature response to "Louisa, Please Come Home."**

Student Model

A Literature Response to
"Louisa, Please Come Home"

by Maureen Ryan

A time when I felt misunderstood like Louisa was last year in math class. My teacher recognized me because she had taught my older brother the year before. First, she compared me to him. She said she expected me to do as well in math as he had. When I didn't get good grades, she said I should drop the drama club to study math more. But the drama club is an important part of my identity. Finally, I talked to my teacher about this problem. I explained that I wanted her to get to know me and my unique qualities. Like Louisa, I didn't want to be misunderstood.

Parts of a Literature Response

▶ **Find these parts of Maureen's literature response.**

1. Underline the sentence that **relates the writer's experience** to Louisa.

2. Check three important **details** that describe the experience.

3. Number these details in the **time order** they happened.

4. Circle the **linking words** that connect the details.

5. Put a star before the sentence that **sums up** the writer's ideas and feelings.

Brainstorm

▶ Read the writing prompt at the top of the idea web. Then use the boxes to help you brainstorm your ideas.

Writing Prompt:
Tell about a time when you felt totally misunderstood, like Louisa.

At School

With Friends

In Your Family

With Other People

Plan Your Paragraph

Writing Prompt: Tell about a time when you felt totally misunderstood, like Louisa.

▶ **Use this chart to plan and organize your paragraph.**

Word Choices
_____
_____
_____
_____
_____

Introduce the Topic

• *A time when . . .*

• *Like Louisa, I . . .*

• *There was a time when . . .*

Detail 1

• *First, . . .*

• *First of all, . . .*

• *It all started when . . .*

Detail 2

• *When . . .*

• *Next, . . .*

• *After that, . . .*

Detail 3

• *Finally, . . .*

• *In the end, . . .*

• *It got better after . . .*

Conclusion

• *That's why . . .*

• *I felt like . . .*

• *Overall, I felt . . .*

Write Your Paragraph

▶ Use this writing frame to write a first draft of your paragraph.

_____ (title)

A time when _____

_____

_____

_____

First, _____

_____

_____

_____

When _____

_____

_____

_____

Finally, _____

_____

_____

_____

That's why _____

_____

_____

_____

Revise

▶ Rate your paragraph. Then have a writing partner rate it.

Scoring Guide			
weak	okay	good	strong
1	2	3	4

1. Does the beginning **relate the writer's experience** to Louisa?

| Self | 1 | 2 | 3 | 4 |
| Partner | 1 | 2 | 3 | 4 |

2. Are there **details** that describe the experience?

| Self | 1 | 2 | 3 | 4 |
| Partner | 1 | 2 | 3 | 4 |

3. Are the details arranged in the **time order** they happened?

| Self | 1 | 2 | 3 | 4 |
| Partner | 1 | 2 | 3 | 4 |

4. Do **linking words** connect the details?

| Self | 1 | 2 | 3 | 4 |
| Partner | 1 | 2 | 3 | 4 |

5. Does the ending **sum up** the writer's ideas and feelings?

| Self | 1 | 2 | 3 | 4 |
| Partner | 1 | 2 | 3 | 4 |

▶ Now revise your paragraph to make it stronger.

Grammar CORRECTING RUN-ON SENTENCES

A run-on sentence is made up of two complete thoughts that are incorrectly joined together.

- To fix a run-on sentence, separate the ideas into two complete sentences.
- Or, insert a comma and a connecting word between the thoughts.

Example

Run-on sentence: Louisa lived here she ran away.

Complete sentences: Louisa lived here. She ran away.
Complete sentence: Louisa lived here, but she ran away.

▶ **Put an R next to the run-on sentences. Put a C next to the complete sentences.**

1. Louisa chose that day she wanted to ruin the wedding.   _____R_____

2. We miss our daughter she disappeared.   _____

3. No one stopped her Paul saw her leave.   _____

4. She got a good job when she reached Chandler.   _____

5. Mrs. Peacock was glad that Louisa saved some money.   _____

6. Louisa didn't miss her family she saw Paul again.   _____

▶ **Rewrite the run-on sentences below as complete sentences.**

7. Her mother didn't recognize her they had both changed.

_____

8. Even Louisa's father didn't know her he tried to be nice.

_____

9. He gave Louisa money she gave it to Paul.

_____

10. This story was depressing Louisa made some poor choices.

_____

Edit ➤ *Take a close look at each of the sentences in your draft on page 77. Are any of them run-on sentences? If so, fix them.*

Usage USING CORRECT WORD ORDER

The **order of words** in a sentence must make sense.

- An adjective comes before the noun it describes.
- A helping verb comes just before the main verb in a statement.

Example

Correct	Incorrect
Louisa bought a new coat.	Louisa bought a coat new.
I know where Louisa is going.	I know where is Louisa going.

▶ **Find and correct five errors in this paragraph.**

Student Model

Like Louisa, I have felt misunderstood. In seventh grade, was I learning how to play the drums. They became a big part of my idintity. My best friend was getting into sports. He couldn't recognise what music meant to me. He said some cruel things he thought I was wasting my time. He didn't really know me anymore. Like Louisa, I wanted to start a life new with new friends.

Check and Correct

- ☐ Circle two spelling errors and correct them.
- ☐ Underline two word order errors and correct them.
- ☐ Correct one run-on sentence.

 Edit Look at the sentences in your own draft on page 77. Do they all use correct word order? If not, fix them.

Final Draft /Present

▶ **Write a final draft of your paragraph on paper or the computer. Check it again and correct any errors before you present it.**

Meet the Author

SHIRLEY JACKSON

Shirley Jackson 1916–1965

" *In times of stress . . . we are revealed in our true personalities.* "

From the time she was a little girl, Shirley Jackson knew she wanted to be a writer. At age twelve, she won her first poetry contest. In high school, she kept a diary about her stories. And in college, she wrote for the school magazine. But during college, Jackson became very sick. Writing was the only thing that made her feel better. She would write a thousand words every day.

Finally, Jackson's hard work paid off. She became famous. It seemed like nothing could stop her. She became well known for her stories with creepy plots and shocking endings. Then, her health became worse. Shirley Jackson died in 1965. She left a collection of stories that readers everywhere love to talk about.

Famous Stories:
"The Lottery"
"After You, My Dear Alphonse"
"Charles"

Ask Yourself

1. **Underline** ▷ How old was Jackson when she won her first writing contest?

2. **Circle** ▷ What was the only thing that made Jackson feel better?

3. Do you like stories with shocking endings? Explain.

_____

_____

_____

_____

Evaluating a Book Review

How can you tell if you will like a book? You can read a review of it. A book review gives a summary of the book. It also gives the reviewer's opinion. Read this review of *Among the Hidden* by Margaret Peterson Haddix.

Among the Hidden is a great novel. The book is full of suspense. You are always surprised at what happens. The story is set in the future. The Government has laws about how many children a family can have. It is illegal to have more than two children. Since Luke is the third child in his family, he has had to spend his entire life in hiding. If anyone finds out about him, the Population Police will punish his whole family.

Luke discovers that the new neighbors have a third child, too. Her name is Jen. Luke sneaks over to her house to meet her. There he learns that Jen has been organizing a rally of hidden children. She urges Luke to attend. Will he be brave enough to go?

This story is unforgettable. The characters are realistic and brave. Anyone who reads this book won't be able to put it down.

▶ **Fill in the circle next to each correct answer.**

1. What was the reviewer's opinion of the book?
   - Ⓐ She thought it was not believable.
   - Ⓑ She thought it was poorly written.
   - Ⓒ She thought it was a great story.
   - Ⓓ She loved reading about the future.

2. What is the book about?
   - Ⓐ a boy in hiding
   - Ⓑ protest rallies
   - Ⓒ a mean neighbor
   - Ⓓ unfair parents

3. Which of these is a fact about the story?
   - Ⓐ The story is boring.
   - Ⓑ The story is too long.
   - Ⓒ The story takes place in the future.
   - Ⓓ The story is too babyish.

4. Does the reviewer think you will like this book?
   - Ⓐ yes
   - Ⓑ no
   - Ⓒ She's not sure.
   - Ⓓ She doesn't care.

5. Which is a reason to read a book review?
   - Ⓐ to find out how the story ends
   - Ⓑ to find out how much the book costs
   - Ⓒ to find out if the book is at the library
   - Ⓓ to find out if other people liked the book

Comprehension

▶ **Fill in the circle next to the correct answer.**

1. In "Louisa, Please Come Home," when does Louisa run away?

Ⓐ her birthday

Ⓑ New Year's Day

Ⓒ her sister's wedding day

Ⓓ the day before her sister's wedding

2. Which pair of words best describes Paul?

Ⓐ loud and smart

Ⓑ humble and brave

Ⓒ sneaky and cruel

Ⓓ funny and irresponsible

Here's a tip.
For short-answer
questions, restate the
question in your answer.
This helps focus your
answer.

3. How does Louisa deal with the problem of her parents not recognizing her?

Ⓐ She turns on the radio.

Ⓑ She marries Paul.

Ⓒ She goes back to her new life.

Ⓓ She proves her identity.

4. Which of these will most likely happen in the future?

Ⓐ Louisa will prove her identity to her parents.

Ⓑ Louisa will quit her job.

Ⓒ Louisa will call her sister.

Ⓓ Louisa will keep living with Mrs. Peacock.

5. How are the two poems on pages 70–71 similar?

Ⓐ They are both about Louisa.

Ⓑ They are both about identity.

Ⓒ They are both about frogs.

Ⓓ They are both about going to school.

Vocabulary

▶ **Fill in the circle next to the correct definition of the underlined word.**

1. Louisa didn't look <u>unique</u>, so she blended in with the crowd.
   - Ⓐ special and one of a kind
   - Ⓑ like all the others
   - Ⓒ old-fashioned
   - Ⓓ modern

2. Paul had no trouble <u>recognizing</u> Louisa.
   - Ⓐ thinking she was someone else
   - Ⓑ not understanding who she was
   - Ⓒ knowing who she was
   - Ⓓ all of the above

3. Louisa's parents thought she was another <u>impostor</u>.
   - Ⓐ a person who is unkind
   - Ⓑ a person who is a twin
   - Ⓒ a person who pretends to be someone else
   - Ⓓ a person who always tells the truth

▶ **Choose the correct form of the underlined verb.**

4. Paul had <u>deceive</u> Louisa's family before.
   - Ⓐ deceived
   - Ⓑ deceives
   - Ⓒ deceiving
   - Ⓓ correct as is

▶ **Choose the correct word to fill in the blank.**

5. When Louisa moved to Chandler, she changed her _____.
   - Ⓐ idea
   - Ⓑ identify
   - Ⓒ identity
   - Ⓓ identical

Short Answer

▶ **Use what you've read in this Workshop to answer the question below. Check your spelling and grammar.**

Would you want to be Louisa's friend? Why or why not?

_____

_____

_____

_____

_____

WORKSHOP 4

NONFICTION

Comprehension Focus
Summarize

READINGS
1 *Life in the Dumps* >> Newspaper Article
2 *Working in the Fields* >> Magazine Article
3 *Child Labor Around the World* >> Social Studies Text

Stolen Childhoods

Around the world, nearly 250 million children work for a living. From Mexico to Pakistan, they slave away on farms, in factories, and even in garbage dumps. These kids don't go to school. For most of them, school isn't even an option.

Why must kids work? What is being done to help them get back their childhoods?

VOCABULARY BUILDER

◎ Target Word ▶ Read the Target Words. Rate each one using the scale below.*	Meaning ▶ Read the Target Word meanings. Write in the missing ones.	Example ▶ Finish the Target Word examples below. Write in the missing ones.
benefit *be•ne•fit* *(noun)* ① ② ③		One benefit of playing a sport is . . .
economy *e•con•o•my* *(noun)* ① ② ③	the way money is made and shared	
international *in•ter•na•tion•al* *(adjective)* ① ② ③		Child labor is an **international** problem. It happens all over the world.
labor *la•bor* *(noun)* ① ② ③	hard work	
produce *pro•duce* *(verb)* ① ② ③		An electronics factory produces . . .

*Rating Scale
①= I don't know it at all.
②= I've seen it before.
③= I know it and use it.

The Big Idea

Write What is this article mainly about?

_____

_____

_____

VOCABULARY BUILDER
Target Word

require

re•quire (verb)

Rate it: ① ② ③

Meaning

_____

_____

Example

_____

_____

_____

React

Imagine that you could make laws and rules. What laws would you make to help kids like Tariah?

Life in the Dumps
Children Work Long Days Sifting Through Garbage

May 10, 2003—Every day, more than 600 children pick through mountains of garbage at the dump in Bekasi, Indonesia. Eleven-year-old Tariah is one of them.

Tariah does manual labor for a living. Every day, she picks through piles of rotting trash. Flies swarm around her head. Huge bulldozers roar nearby. Thick, dirty smoke stings her eyes.

Tariah hunts for tattered plastic bags. She also looks for scrap metal. Tariah's tiny hands bleed from touching broken glass. At the end of the day, she gives the trash to her boss. He resells it to recycling companies.

Tariah's job **requires** backbreaking work, but she earns only pennies a day. She gives the money to her parents. They need it for their family to survive.

A young girl in Indonesia works in a garbage dump.

Tariah wants to leave the dump. "I'm learning to read and write," she says. "I want to be a teacher."

Like Tariah, kids all over the world work in dumps. It's an international problem. These kids work for 9 to 12 hours a day. The lucky ones earn $16 a month. But they all lose much more. They miss out on school. They get sick. They don't have any fun. Worst of all, they have lost their childhoods. END

Words to Know! **manual** by hand

Comprehension Focus
Summarize

A **summary** is a short statement of the most important ideas in a reading. To summarize:

- Find the topic of the text.
- Look for the most important details about the topic.
- Restate the topic and important details in a short summary. Use your own words.

▶ **Fill in this chart with the topic and important details in "Life in the Dumps."**

Topic

_____

_____

_____

Details

1. _Eleven-year-old Tariah picks through piles of rotting trash._

_____

2. _____

_____

3. _____

_____

Summarize

▶ **Now summarize the article. Check that you:**
- ☐ state the topic
- ☐ give important details about the topic
- ☐ use your own words

The Big Idea

Write ▶ What is this article mainly about?

_____

_____

_____

border

bor•der (noun)

Rate it: ① ② ③

Meaning

_____

_____

Example

_____

_____

_____

_____

React

What do you do during your summer vacation? How does it compare to what James Flores does?

WORKING IN THE FIELDS

Across America, teens work in the fields, picking the crops that feed us

In the United States, nearly 150,000 teens are migrant workers. They travel from field to field, picking crops. These teens work in the sweltering heat. They sacrifice their time and freedom. They do it to help their families.

Summer Days

For the last seven years, James Flores has spent summers on a farm in Ohio. But James is not on vacation. He's working. The farm produces fruits and vegetables. James picks crops to help his family make ends meet. He works nine hours a day, six days a week. That's 54 hours—14 hours over the legal limit for kids.

In the U.S., teens work in the sweltering heat for little pay.

Sometimes James carries 50 pounds of cucumbers at a time. "The weight is heavy," says the 14-year-old. "It's hard to take. But the hardest part is not having fun. I'd rather be playing than working."

Crossing the Border

Many teens come from other countries to find work in the U.S. Why? They want to help their families back home. In their home countries, families earn barely enough to get by.

Many of these workers come here legally. But some cross our **borders** illegally. Seventeen-year-old Rodrigo Perez comes here illegally. He is from Guatemala. He works on a farm in Massachusetts. To get to his job, Rodrigo has to travel over 2,200 miles.

Rodrigo works hard at his job, but he earns little more than the minimum wage. He doesn't even keep the money for himself. He sends most of his pay home to Guatemala. "I send money to help my family live better," he says.

Rodrigo isn't alone. Between 60 and 80 percent of migrant workers are from other countries. Together, these workers send millions of dollars home to Latin America and the Caribbean. ➡

| Words to Know! | **sacrifice** to give up |

1. [Write]▷ What is the topic of the section "Summer Days"?

_____

_____

_____

_____

_____

2. [Underline]▷ Find two details in "Summer Days" that relate to the topic.

3. Summarize the section in your own words. Tell your summary to a partner.

4. [Write]▷ What is the topic of the section "Crossing the Border"?

_____

_____

_____

_____

5. [Underline]▷ Find two details in "Crossing the Border" that relate to the topic.

6. Summarize the section in your own words. Tell your summary to a partner.

Active Reading

Underline ▸ Why does Jessica give her father half of her wages?

VOCABULARY BUILDER
Target Word

resources

re•sourc•es (noun)

Rate it: ①   ②   ③

Meaning

_____

_____

Example

_____

_____

_____

 React

Write ▸ Do you think that kids in the U.S. should do farm labor? Why or why not?

_____

_____

_____

_____

Families Working Together

Many U.S. teens do farm labor alongside their families. Half of these families earn less than $10,000 a year. Mothers, fathers, and children must all work to pay the bills.

Fourteen-year-old Jessica Roman works with her father and brothers. She picks blueberries all day long. It is exhausting work. But she gives half her wages to her father. The money helps pay the family's bills.

James Flores works with his parents, two sisters, and eight brothers. "I feel proud to make money to help support my family," James says.

"Many migrant children help feed and clothe the family," says Jeanne Cure. She works for a group that helps migrant families. Workers get paid by the amount they pick, Cure explains. "If their kids help, it

"I feel proud to make money to help support my family," James says.

means more hands picking."

A Better Life

What can be done to help young field workers? The Migrant Education Program offers many **resources**, such as free tutoring and health services.

Rodrigo is one of 620,000 youth currently in the program. He goes to classes four nights a week.

"I go because I want to learn English," he says. "I want a better life." **END**

A girl picks grapes in a California field.

Words to Know!   **exhausting** very tiring

Comprehension Focus
Summarize

▶ Fill in this chart with the topic and important details in "Working in the Fields."

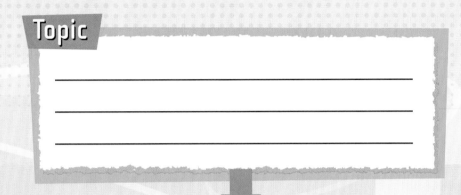

Topic

_____

_____

_____

Details

1. _____

_____

_____

2. _____

_____

_____

3. _____

_____

_____

Summarize

▶ Now tell your summary to a partner.
Check that you:

☐ state the topic

☐ give important details about the topic

☐ use your own words

The Big Idea

Write What is this article mainly about?

_____

_____

_____

VOCABULARY BUILDER

Target Word

deprive

de•prive (verb)

Rate it: ① ② ③

Meaning

_____

_____

Example

_____

_____

_____

 React

Would you use a soccer ball that a young child stitched up? Why or why not?

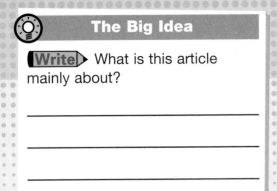

CHILD LABOR
Around the World

From dusty farms to hot factories, kids slave away. They earn only pennies a day.

A Global Problem

Around the world, nearly 250 million children work for a living. They spend their days on farms and in factories. Some work full-time. Others work part-time. But they all work for very little pay. These children are **deprived** of a normal childhood. They can't even go to school. The only benefit of their jobs is the little money they give to their parents.

Child labor is a global problem. In Brazil, close to 150,000 children pick oranges. They work in extreme heat for 14 hours a day. Their fingertips are blistered from pesticides. In Pakistan, close to 12 million children stitch together soccer balls and sportswear. Some are as young as five years old. And in Indonesia, teens suffer in hot, stuffy factories. They lace up $100 tennis shoes for only 15 cents an hour.

Words to Know! **statistic** number

This child's job is to stitch together soccer balls.

Real Kids, Real Lives

These kids aren't just statistics. They have faces and names—just like you.

Bonauli works seven days a week on a fishing pier in Indonesia. He rarely sees his family. "I miss my mom," he says. But his mother lives very far away.

In Istanbul, Turkey, 11-year-old Mushin sells travel packages of tissues on a street corner. His customers are taxi drivers. Mushin goes from car to car when they stop at traffic lights. On a good day, Mushin sells enough to buy a handful of crackers for lunch.

Eleven-year-old Muhammad works on a tea farm in India. From 5 A.M. until 9:30 P.M. he picks tea leaves. "My boss beats me," he says. "It is my dream, for just one day, to go to school."

Thousands of kids around the world feel like Muhammad. But their dreams may never come true. ➡

Summarize

1. **Write** What is the topic of "A Global Problem"?

_____

_____

_____

_____

2. **Underline** Find two details in "A Global Problem" that relate to the topic.

3. Summarize the section in your own words. Tell your summary to a partner.

4. **Write** What is the topic of "Real Kids, Real Lives"?

_____

_____

_____

_____

5. **Underline** Find two details in "Real Kids, Real Lives" that relate to the topic.

6. Summarize the section in your own words. Tell your summary to a partner.

Review: Sequence

Circle In the section "Real Kids, Real Lives" when does Muhammad work?

Active Reading

Star What happened when school fees were banned in Kenya?

VOCABULARY BUILDER
Target Word

reform

re•form (verb)

Rate it: ① ② ③

Meaning

_____

_____

Example

_____

_____

_____

React

Write Do you think education should be free for all children everywhere? Why or why not?

_____

_____

_____

_____

_____

From Work to School

There are many complicated reasons why children must work. In Kenya, the problem began in 1982. During that year, the country was faced with major debts. To pay them, the government decided to charge a fee to attend school. Families had to pay up to $350 per year. This was a huge amount of money in Kenya's economy. On average, Kenyans make only $1 a day. School became a luxury. Few could afford it.

Most parents couldn't pay the school fee. Instead, they sent their kids to work. Many children were sent to pick coffee beans in dangerous conditions. In 2002, 4 million Kenyan kids worked instead of going to school.

Finally, in 2003, the Kenyan government banned the school fees. Overnight, school enrollment boomed. One and a half million kids showed up to learn.

Words to Know! **luxury** something very rich and special

 TEXT FEATURE **Reading a Time Line**

Key Events in Child Labor History

1938
The Fair Labor Standards Act—establishing child labor standards in the U.S.—is signed into law.

1943
Because of World War II, child labor laws are relaxed to allow teenagers to work in wartime factories.

1989
The United Nations unanimously adopts the Convention on the Rights of the Child, which spells out the basic human right of children around the world.

1995
Iqbal Masih, a former child slave turned child labor activist, is murdered.

2004
The Children's World Congress holds the first ever global youth congress on child labor in Florence, Italy. Five hundred kids, aged 10 to 17, gather to share their perspectives on child labor.

Ending Child Labor

Experts around the world agree. Education is the key to ending child labor. But even in Kenya, only elementary school is free. High school costs money. In many other nations, there is no free public education.

Many people are working together to **reform** child labor. The United Nations assists children who work by giving them food and medicine. In the U.S., many citizens protest products made by child labor. Their goal is clear—to end child labor for good. (END)

Kids in Kenya can now go to school for free.

A time line shows key events in history.

1. When was the Fair Labor Standards Act signed into law?
   Ⓐ 1938   Ⓑ 1943
   Ⓒ 1995   Ⓓ 2004

2. What happened to U.S. child labor laws in 1943?
   Ⓐ They were approved by the U.N.
   Ⓑ They were protested by a group of 500 kids.
   Ⓒ They were relaxed to allow teens to work in factories.
   Ⓓ Ten-year-olds were allowed to work in schools.

3. How many years after Iqbal Masih's death did the Children's World Congress meet?

   _____

 Summarize

1. **Write** What is the topic of the section "From Work to School"?

   _____

   _____

   _____

2. **Underline** Find two details in "From Work to School" that relate to the topic.

3. Summarize the section in your own words. Tell your summary to a partner.

Skills Check

1. **Write** What is the topic of the section "Ending Child Labor"?

   _____

   _____

   _____

2. **Underline** Find two details in "Ending Child Labor" that relate to the topic.

3. Write a summary of this section on a separate sheet of paper.

TAKE THE WORD CHALLENGE

Start

1 **Circle one in each row.** Would you rather be deprived of . . .

television **OR** video games?

friends **OR** family?

radio music **OR** music videos?

sleep **OR** food?

2 **List them.** You just won an international trip to three countries. Which countries would you visit?

1. _____

2. _____

3. _____

Now pick three international cities you'd like to visit.

1. _____

2. _____

3. _____

3 **Using a Dictionary**
Guide words are the words on the top of dictionary pages. They tell the first and last words listed on those pages.

Write these Target Words next to the words that could be their guide words:

international	labor	produce

Guide words	Target Words
problematic, profitability	_____
internal, intro	_____
know, ladder	_____

marsupial ▶ mass media

mask (mask)
1. noun A covering worn over the face to hide, protect, or disguise it. This mask, made in New Guinea, would have been worn by a boy at a special ceremony to celebrate his adulthood. ▷ **adjective masked**
2. verb To cover up or disguise something. A smile masked his actual disgust. ▷ **masking, masked** ▷ **noun mask**
ma·son (may-suhn) **noun** Someone who builds or works with stone, cement, or bricks.

4 **You choose.** Your school just got money for a new resource. Which do you vote for?

☐ a gym with a pool and a weight room

☐ a student lounge with comfortable couches

☐ a health center with a full-time nurse and doctor

☐ a recording studio for musicians and singers

5 **Check it.** Which of these would you most like to produce someday?

☐ some cool music

☐ some great art

☐ an action movie

☐ other: _____

_____

_____

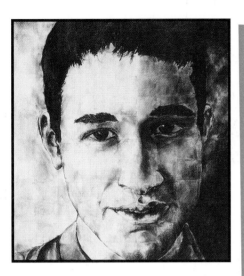

6 Rate it.
Rate it. Which of these tasks would require the most labor for you? Rate these from 1 to 4.
1 = requires the least labor
4 = requires the most labor

____ drawing a self-portrait

____ cooking a dinner for four

____ baby-sitting eight kids

____ cleaning up your school

7 Think about it.
Think about it.
List some benefits of being famous.

_____

_____

_____

_____

What would not be a benefit of being famous?

_____

_____

8 Multiple-Meaning Words

Multiple-meaning words are words that have more than one meaning.

Read the definitions of these multiple-meaning words. Use them to fill in the blanks below.

benefit: 1. *(noun)* a good result
        2. *(noun)* a performance to raise money for a charity

bowl: 1. *(noun)* a round container
       2. *(verb)* to roll a heavy ball toward pins

track: 1. *(noun)* a narrow road or path
        2. *(verb)* to search

a bowl of popcorn

bowling ball

• Detectives followed the train _____,

  hoping to _____ down the thief.

• One _____ of having a _____ is raising

  money for a good cause.

• Tyra loves to _____, especially if she can snack on

  a _____ of popcorn at the same time.

9 Evaluate.
Evaluate. Read each statement. Write **A** for agree, and **D** for disagree. Be ready to defend your point of view.

____ Laws against street skateboarding should be reformed.

____ School rules about dress codes should be reformed.

____ Laws that say drivers must be 16 or older must be reformed.

10 Fill in.
Fill in. Complete these sentences with either border or economy.

• I contribute to the

  _____

  by buying one CD a week.

• My annoying brother and I share a room. We drew a

  _____

  down the middle, separating his half from mine.

Finish

Writing Focus
Expository Summary

A **summary** gives the most important ideas and details from a reading.

▶ **Read Luis's summary of "Life in the Dumps."**

Student Model

Summary of "Life in the Dumps"
by Luis Hernandez

"Life in the Dumps" describes the international problem of child labor. First, it explains the story of 11-year-old Tariah. She has to sift through rotting trash at a garbage dump so she can support her family. Then, the article explains that Tariah is learning to read and write so she can quit working at the dump. Finally, we learn that there are children like Tariah all over the world. They have all been deprived of their childhoods.

Parts of an Expository Summary
▶ **Find these parts of Luis's expository summary paragraph.**

1. Underline the sentence that states the **topic of the reading**.
2. Check three **important details**.
3. Circle the **linking words** that connect the details.
4. Reread to see that the summary is in the **writer's own words**.
5. Decide if the summary is **brief, but complete**.

Brainstorm

▶ Read the writing prompt in the middle of the idea web. Then use the boxes to help you organize your ideas.

Important Detail

Important Detail

Writing Prompt:
Write a paragraph that summarizes the article "Working in the Fields."

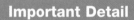

Important Detail

Important Detail

Plan Your Paragraph

Writing Prompt: Write a paragraph that summarizes the article "Working in the Fields."

▶ **Use this chart to plan and organize your paragraph.**

Word Choices

_____

_____

_____

_____

_____

Topic

- *The article "Working in the Fields" . . .*

- *Migrant workers in the United States . . .*

- *"Working in the Fields" describes . . .*

First Important Detail

- *First, it explains . . .*

- *During the summer, . . .*

- *The big issue . . .*

Second Important Detail

- *Then, . . .*

- *Next, . . .*

- *In addition, . . .*

Third Important Detail

- *It also . . .*

- *The main reason . . .*

- *Their families . . .*

Last Important Detail

- *Finally, . . .*

- *The last important point is that . . .*

- *In summary . . .*

Write Your Paragraph

▶ Use this writing frame to write a first draft of your paragraph.

The article "Working in the Fields" describes _____

_____

_____

_____

First, it explains _____

_____

_____

_____

Then, _____

_____

_____

_____

It also _____

_____

_____

_____

Finally, _____

_____

_____

_____

_____

Revise

▶ Rate your paragraph. Then have a writing partner rate it.

Scoring Guide			
weak	okay	good	strong
1	2	3	4

1. Does the first sentence state the **topic of the reading**?

Self	1	2	3	4
Partner	1	2	3	4

2. Does the summary contain only **important details**?

Self	1	2	3	4
Partner	1	2	3	4

3. Do **linking words** connect the details?

Self	1	2	3	4
Partner	1	2	3	4

4. Is the summary written in the **writer's own words**?

Self	1	2	3	4
Partner	1	2	3	4

5. Is the summary **brief, yet complete**?

Self	1	2	3	4
Partner	1	2	3	4

▶ Now revise your paragraph to make it stronger.

Grammar USING CORRECT VERB TENSE

The **tense** of a verb shows when the action happens.

- A **present-tense verb** shows action that is happening now.

- A **past-tense verb** shows action that took place in the past. Most past-tense verbs end in *-ed*.

Example

Present-Tense Verb	Past-Tense Verb
James works on a farm.	James worked on a farm last summer.
James picks fruit.	James picked fruit yesterday.

▶ **Identify the tense of the verb in each sentence below by writing present or past on the line to the right.**

1. Tariah worked in the garbage dump.　　　　*past*

2. Migrant farmers produce food for many people.　　　　_____

3. The families worked in the sun all day.　　　　_____

4. James carried piles of cucumbers every day.　　　　_____

5. Muhammad sells tissues to cab drivers.　　　　_____

6. He misses his grandparents very much.　　　　_____

▶ **Rewrite the sentences below using the past tense of the verb.**

7. Rodrigo travels from Guatemala to the U.S.

_____

8. He works on a farm in the U.S.

_____

9. The migrant workers earn little money.

_____

10. Tutors help young farm workers.

_____

 Edit　*Take a close look at each of the sentences in your draft on page 101. Do they all use correct verb tense? Fix the ones that don't.*

Mechanics USING COMMAS IN A SERIES

Items in a series are separated by **commas**.

- A series is a list of the same kinds of words.
- Commas follow every item in the series except the last one.

Example

Correct	Incorrect
Snakebites, cuts, and other injuries are part of the job.	Snakebites cuts and other injuries are part of the job.

▶ **Find and correct five errors in this paragraph.**

Student Model

The article "Life in the Dumps" describes the problem of child laber in dumps. First, it tells Tariah's story. She sifts through trash looking for scrap metal glass and plastic bags. Then, it explains how she must sell the garbage. This supported her family. Finally, it explains how child labor is an internashonal problem.

Check and Correct

☐ Circle two spelling errors and correct them.

☐ Insert two missing commas.

☐ Correct one verb-tense error.

 Edit Look at the sentences in your own draft on page 101. Do they all use commas in a series correctly? Fix the ones that don't.

Final Draft/Present

▶ **Write a final draft of your paragraph on paper or the computer. Check it again and correct any errors before you present it.**

Factory Worker

Newspapers print articles about issues like child labor. They are produced in a newspaper plant. Adrian Salazar helps print *The Houston Chronicle*. All night long, he makes sure the paper is printing properly. In the morning, the newspapers are delivered all over the Houston area. "It's cool to pick up a newspaper the next day and look at the quality of my work," Adrian says.

Adrian Salazar helps print *The Houston Chronicle*.

Name: Adrian Salazar

Hometown: Houston, Texas

Job: Newspaper plant worker

Duties:
- fills press with ink
- sets up the printing press
- checks the color quality
- prints the newspaper

Skills:
- physical and mental energy for night and weekend work
- knowledge of computer control panel
- ability to evaluate printed colors and correct color measurements

Similar Jobs:
- machine setter or operator
- car factory worker

Pay: $18.00 per hour

Education: High School Diploma

Ask Yourself

1. **Underline** How much education does this job require?

2. **Circle** When does Adrian work—during the day or at night?

3. How much do you want this job?
   - ❏ I don't want it.
   - ❏ I might want it.
   - ❏ I really want it.

Filling Out a Job Form

When Adrian started his job, he had to fill out a form with the Human Resources Department where he worked. This form stays on record so that the company can send Adrian his paycheck and contact someone if there's an emergency. Fill out the form below for practice.

Welcome to Our Company!

Please fill out this information about yourself for our records.

(Print) First Name	Middle Name	Last Name

Date of Birth	Gender

Home Telephone Number	Cell Phone Number

Home Address (Street Number)

City	State	Zip

Mailing Address (Street Number)

City	State	Zip

Emergency Contact	Relationship

Home Telephone Number	Cell Phone Number

Second Emergency Contact	Relationship

Home Telephone Number	Cell Phone Number

Our company encourages volunteering. List three groups or activities you would be interested in volunteering for: _____

_____

_____

Comprehension

▶ **Fill in the circle next to the correct answer.**

1. Children who work in dumps look mainly for _____.

- Ⓐ toys and old clothing
- Ⓑ cucumbers and blueberries
- Ⓒ scrap metal and plastic bags
- Ⓓ coffee beans

2. In the U.S, there are an estimated _____ teens who are migrant workers.

- Ⓐ 150,000
- Ⓑ 50,000,000
- Ⓒ 1,500
- Ⓓ 15,000

Here's a tip.
Look for questions that ask you to give a personal response. These questions require an opinion, not just facts.

3. Which sentence gives the best summary of "Child Labor Around the World"?

- Ⓐ Child labor isn't a widespread problem.
- Ⓑ Child labor only happens in America.
- Ⓒ Child labor is an international problem that needs a solution.
- Ⓓ Child labor is bad, but there's nothing we can do.

4. Why did the Kenyan government start charging money for children to go to school?

- Ⓐ They thought kids would work harder if school wasn't free.
- Ⓑ Because the economy was bad, the Kenyan government needed the money.
- Ⓒ Coffee farmers wanted more kids to work in the fields.
- Ⓓ Schools became very expensive because they had computers.

5. What happened when Kenya made schools free again?

- Ⓐ All the students dropped out.
- Ⓑ Many children stopped working and enrolled in schools.
- Ⓒ Coffee planters protested.
- Ⓓ Students couldn't afford the bus fare to school.

Vocabulary

▶ **Fill in the circle next to the correct definition of the underlined word.**

1. The <u>economy</u> of Kenya is dependent on coffee.
   - Ⓐ the way people enjoy their life
   - Ⓒ the size of the country
   - Ⓑ the way money is made and shared
   - Ⓓ the rainfall

2. Around the world, child <u>labor</u> is a big problem.
   - Ⓐ rest
   - Ⓒ hard work
   - Ⓑ eat
   - Ⓓ have fun

3. Often, <u>international</u> attention can help stop the abuse of child workers.
   - Ⓐ American
   - Ⓒ television
   - Ⓑ from more than one country
   - Ⓓ student

▶ **Choose the correct definition for the underlined multiple-meaning word.**

4. The car factory will no longer <u>produce</u> last year's popular model.
   - Ⓐ eat
   - Ⓒ food
   - Ⓑ suffer from
   - Ⓓ make

▶ **Which are the most likely dictionary guide words for the underlined word?**

5. One <u>benefit</u> of an education is preparation for a good job.
   - Ⓐ *bat* and *batch*
   - Ⓒ *belt* and *bet*
   - Ⓑ *better* and *butter*
   - Ⓓ *drawback* and *bonus*

Short Answer

▶ **Use what you've read in this Workshop to answer the question below. Check your spelling and grammar.**

What do you think the worst thing is about child labor? Why?

_____

_____

_____

_____

_____

WORKSHOP 5

NONFICTION

Comprehension Focus
Problem and Solution

READINGS
1 *Tragic Death on Train* >> Newspaper Article
2 *The Secrets of Self-Esteem* >> Magazine Article
3 *The Power of Peer Pressure* >> Life Skills Feature

UNDER PRESSURE

Being a teenager is tough. From ages 12 to 14, teens are under serious pressure from their peers. It's not always easy to handle.

Sometimes teens pressure each other into doing bad things. They do dangerous stunts. They make fun of the unpopular kids. Sometimes they really hurt each other.

You have to make the choice. It's not an easy one. Can you take the pressure?

VOCABULARY BUILDER

◎ Target Word ▶ Read the Target Words. Rate each one using the scale below.*	Meaning ▶ Read the Target Word meanings. Write in the missing ones.	Example ▶ Finish the Target Word examples below. Write in the missing ones.
authority au•thor•i•ty (noun) ① ② ③		I'm a top **authority** on fashion.
convince con•vince (verb) ① ② ③	to make someone believe or do something	
image im•age (noun) ① ② ③		The image I want to have at school is . . .
negative neg•a•tive (adjective) ① ② ③	bad	
pressure pres•sure (noun) ① ② ③		At home, I get pressure to . . .

*Rating Scale
① = I don't know it at all.
② = I've seen it before.
③ = I know it and use it.

The Big Idea

Write What is this article mainly about?

_____

_____

_____

_____

VOCABULARY BUILDER
Target Word

rebel

re•bel *(verb)*

Rate it: ① ② ③

Meaning

_____

_____

_____

Example

_____

_____

_____

React

Is peer pressure really to blame for Eric's death? Or is Eric himself to blame? What do you think?

Tragic Death on Train
Peer Pressure Costs Teen His Life

October 26, 2003— For Eric Alvarez, keeping up a cool image was more important than anything— even his safety. Peer pressure was a problem that cost him his life.

Eric rode the subway home from school every day. For fun, his friends pried open the doors of the speeding cars. They would lean out into the tunnels. Eric played along.

Eric's aunt knew what he was doing. She warned him to stop. "It's better to be called a chicken," she said. Eric **rebelled**—and did something even worse.

Last Monday, Eric really wanted to impress his friends. He decided to "surf" the subway. Eric's girlfriend tried to stop him. "Don't do it!" she begged. Again, Eric didn't listen.

Eric climbed to the roof of a speeding car. His head hit a beam. He fell— dead—onto the tracks.

Eric's uncle is sure that peer pressure was to blame. "His friends pressured him to do it," he said.

These same friends attended Eric's funeral. Many had also "surfed" trains. A speaker at the funeral offered a solution. Teens need to fight against negative peer pressure, the man said. Crazy stunts aren't worth it. Peer pressure can kill. *END*

Eric Alvarez in a school photo.

Words to Know! **impress** to make someone admire something

Problem and Solution

A **problem** is a situation or event that causes trouble. A **solution** is what fixes the problem. To find the problem and the solution:

- Look for the problem.
- Look for attempts to solve the problem.
- Find the solution.

▶ **Fill in this chart with the problem and solution in "Tragic Death on Train."**

Problem

Peer pressure led Eric to do dangerous subway stunts with his friends.

Attempts

1. _____

_____

_____

2. _____

_____

_____

Solution

_____

_____

_____

_____

_____

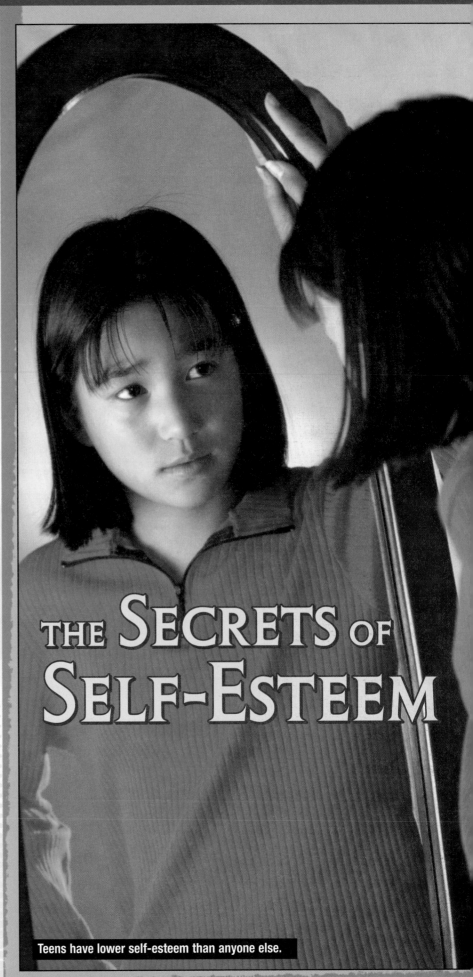

THE SECRETS OF SELF-ESTEEM

Teens have lower self-esteem than anyone else.

Many teens don't respect themselves. It's a big problem. What's the solution?

Many teens are in big trouble. Every day, they deal with a **constant** problem. The problem is pressure that comes from inside themselves. It's called low self-esteem.

Teen Self-Esteem

"Self-esteem" means liking and respecting yourself. People with high self-esteem are comfortable with their unique identities. They know their own strengths and weaknesses. They are proud of who they are.

Authorities say that teens have lower self-esteem than any other age-group. Many teens wish they were more popular or better-looking. They wish they were anything—but themselves.

Looks That Kill

Many teens worry about looking good. They think that looking better will make them happier. Why? Beautiful people are often treated better by others. "Kids in school care about how you look," says 12-year-old Isabel Mendez. "They don't care who you are on the inside."

Some teens try to raise their self-esteem through extreme diets or drugs. They'll do anything to look better.

Girls sometimes think trendy diets will fix their problems. Experts say that 39 percent of girls in fifth to eighth grade are on a diet!

Some boys also have problems with body image. They think the solution is to bulk up. Too many teens take drugs to build muscles.

Diets and drugs aren't solutions. Diets can make you tense and tired. Drugs can damage your body and even kill you. ➡

Problem and Solution

1. **Underline** What is the main problem discussed in this article?

2. **Write** Find two attempts that teens make to solve the problem.

Attempt 1:

_____

_____

_____

_____

_____

Attempt 2:

_____

_____

_____

_____

_____

Active Reading

Underline ▷ Find one way to build your own self-esteem.

VOCABULARY BUILDER

Target Word

appreciate

ap•pre•ci•ate (verb)

Rate it: ③

Meaning

_____

_____

_____

Example

_____

_____

_____

React

Write ▷ What do you like best about yourself?

_____

_____

_____

_____

Strong on the Inside

What *is* the solution to low self-esteem? Try not to focus on things you don't like about yourself. Instead, learn to recognize and **appreciate** the person you are. It's a challenge, but it will work.

Also, remember that you are a teenager. Ask adults about their teen years. Chances are, they'll remember feeling low self-esteem, too. Your self-esteem will improve as you get older.

However, there *are* things you can do today to help yourself feel better. What are they? Check out these tips.

Three Secrets of Self-Esteem

1. Lend a hand. Doing things that benefit others can build your self-esteem. Do you enjoy spending time with kids or the elderly? Are you good with animals? Share your skills. Volunteering can give you a chance to shine.

Helping others can help you feel better about yourself.

2. Find a mentor. Look for someone who can give you good advice. Maybe it's a teacher, a coach, or an older relative. Mentors can help you understand and *deal with* your feelings.

3. Get involved. Find something you like to do. Join a school club. Try out for a sport. Convince your friends to do an activity you think might be fun. Being busy can be a good thing. If you focus on doing something fun, you'll stop focusing on your imperfections.

Lastly, just try to remember one important thing—you won't be a teen forever! **END**

Words to Know! **mentor** someone who offers help and guidance

Problem and Solution

▶ Fill in this chart with the problem, attempts, and solution in "The Secrets of Self-Esteem."

Problem

_____

_____

_____

Attempts

1._____

_____

_____

2._____

_____

_____

Solution

_____

_____

_____

_____

_____

_____

The Big Idea

Write ▶ What is this article mainly about?

_____

_____

_____

_____

principle

prin•ci•ple (noun)

Rate it: ③

Meaning

_____

_____

_____

Example

_____

_____

_____

 React

What would you tell a friend who is being pressured to do something that will make his or her parents really mad?

The Power of PEER PRESSURE

Can you stand up to the crowd?

The Pressure to Fit In

Teens get pressure from all sides. They feel pressure to do well in school, to excel at a sport, or to look really good. But what's the worst kind of pressure? Many teens say it comes from wanting to fit in. That's what peer pressure is all about.

The pressure to fit in is most intense in Grades 6–8. During these years, teens begin to rebel against their families. They start making decisions for themselves. They start to search for **principles**, or beliefs, to live by.

For instance, a teen may decide that her principles include keeping physically fit and alcohol-free. Another teen's principles may involve being loyal to his friends before his family.

For many teens, friends become a *new* family. They join a group and begin to dress like their friends, act like their friends, and even think like their friends. Then the pressure is *really* on!

Experts recommend a solution. Teens need to figure out when peer pressure is healthy—and when it's not.

With Friends Like These . . .

Some teens will do stupid, dangerous things like shoplift or drink just to fit in. But teens aren't stupid. They know their behavior is dangerous. They know it can lead to big trouble. So, why do they do it? Because fitting in is more important than anything.

What are teens to do? First, they need to develop confidence about their values. They need a clear idea of who they are, and who they want to become. Then teens can begin to recognize those qualities in others. They can surround themselves with friends who pressure them in good ways, like joining a sports team. They can avoid friends who pressure them in negative ways, like doing drugs or cutting classes.

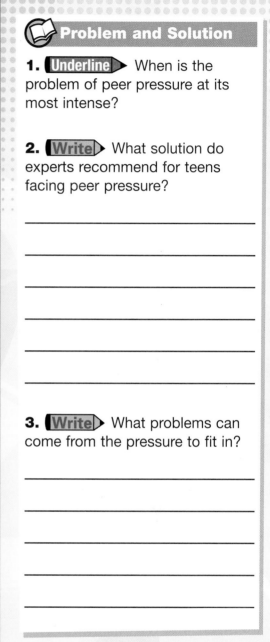

Problem and Solution

1. **Underline** When is the problem of peer pressure at its most intense?

2. **Write** What solution do experts recommend for teens facing peer pressure?

_____

_____

_____

_____

_____

_____

3. **Write** What problems can come from the pressure to fit in?

_____

_____

_____

_____

_____

Review:
Summarize

Find the topic and important details in the section, "With Friends Like These..." Then, turn to a partner and summarize the section.

| **Words to Know!** | **recommend** to suggest a certain action |

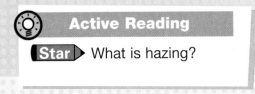

Active Reading

Star What is hazing?

VOCABULARY BUILDER
Target Word

participate

par•ti•ci•pate (verb)

Rate it: ① ② ③

Meaning

_____

_____

_____

Example

_____

_____

_____

React

Write How do your friends influence you? List one good way and one bad way.

Good way: _____

_____

Bad way: _____

_____

Peer Pressure Gets Physical

Hazing is an extreme form of peer pressure. Hazing happens when teens want to join a group. Older teens in the group put the new members through really embarrassing situations. Hazing has become a big problem with clubs and school teams.

In 2003, 15 students in Chicago were charged with assault after a hazing. How did this happen? A group of senior girls invited a group of junior girls to play a football game. The game turned into a hazing. The seniors threw pig intestines and fish guts at the juniors. Girls were beaten, kicked, and choked. In the end, five girls had to be taken to the hospital. One girl had a broken foot and another needed 16 stitches in her head.

The whole incident was caught on video. The video was shown on TV stations all over the country. The school expelled 30 seniors who **participated** in the hazing. The police charged 15 of those girls with battery, which is the legal term for attacking someone. One year later, 10 of the seniors were found guilty. They were sentenced to court supervision and community service.

A few of the juniors who suffered from the hazing hired a lawyer. They filed a 1.5 million dollar lawsuit against the girls who hazed them. The victims hoped that their lawsuit would make other people aware that hazing is a serious problem. They wanted to reinforce the message that hazing is wrong—and must be stopped.

Long-Term Solutions

Why is it so hard for teens to deal with unhealthy peer pressure like hazing? One problem teens have is that they focus on the short term. For example, a teen may feel pressure from friends to smoke. In the short-term, smoking might seem like a solution. But it's not.

Smoking can turn into a long-term problem. It is unhealthy and a hard habit to quit.

A better solution is to think about life in the long term. The next time you are about to do something you may regret, like shoplifting, think in the long term—that stealing is not worth getting a criminal record.

Finally, experts remind teens that peer pressure doesn't last forever. If you can survive Grades 6–8, then you've made it past the hardest part. Until then, stay tough under the pressure! (END)

Words to Know! **reinforce** to make something stronger

TEXT FEATURE **Reading a Bar Graph**

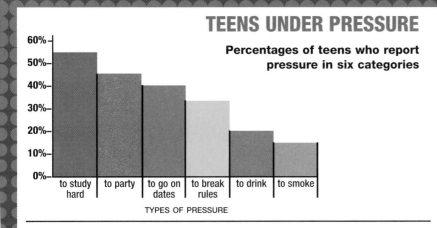

TEENS UNDER PRESSURE

Percentages of teens who report pressure in six categories

TYPES OF PRESSURE

A bar graph shows how different pieces of information relate to each other.

1. What information does this bar graph show?
   - (A) the kinds of teens who feel peer pressure
   - (B) the exact amount of peer pressure a teen feels
   - (C) the percentage of teens who feel different types of pressure

2. What color bar represents the percentage of teens who feel pressured to smoke?
   - (A) green
   - (C) orange
   - (B) blue
   - (D) yellow

3. What percentage of teens say they feel pressure from their peers to go out on dates?

_____

Problem and Solution

1. **Circle** > How do teens get involved with the problem of hazing?

2. **Write** > Find two examples of problems that hazing can cause.

   • _____

   _____

   _____

   • _____

   _____

   _____

Skills Check

1. **Write** > Find an example of a problem that short-term thinking can cause.

   _____

   _____

   _____

   _____

   _____

2. **Underline** > Find an example of how thinking in the long term is a better solution.

TAKE THE WORD CHALLENGE

Start

1 **Check them.** What would give you a negative image at your school?

- ☐ cheating on a final test
- ☐ making fun of other kids
- ☐ riding the school bus
- ☐ wearing ripped-up jeans
- ☐ carrying a skateboard

2 **Check them.** Which of these principles do you agree with?

- ☐ Family comes first.
- ☐ Never turn your back on a friend.
- ☐ Honesty is always the best policy.
- ☐ Don't trust anyone.

3 **Homophones**

Homophones are words that sound alike but have different meanings and spellings. Examples are *peace* and *piece* or *weight* and *wait*.

Match each word to its homophone below.

rode	whole	would

Homophone

hole: _____

road: _____

wood: _____

Fill in the sentence with two homophones.

I was able to _____ my old

_____ phone, and buy a

new one that takes pictures!

Look, I have one guiding **principle**. Always be cool in front of the **principal**.

4 **Fill in.** Finish these sentences.

A coach is an authority on

_____.

A doctor is an authority on

_____.

A DJ is an authority on

_____.

◎ ◎ ◎ ◎ ◎ ◎ ◎ ◎ ◎ ◎ ◎

5 **Check them.** Your friends could probably convince you to:

- ☐ ask someone on a date
- ☐ tell a lie
- ☐ jump off a cliff
- ☐ eat a bug

6 **Check them.** People can rebel in many different ways. Would you ever rebel by:

❏ staying out past curfew

❏ talking to someone who no one else talks to

❏ listening to music no one else likes

❏ wearing strange clothes

7 **Reflect.** It's your birthday. List three gifts you would really appreciate.

1. _____

_____

2. _____

_____

3. _____

_____

8 **Compound Words**

A **compound word** is made up of two smaller words. For example:

Count + down = *countdown*

Draw a line to separate these compound words into two words.

breakdown   downstairs   headache

homework   classmate   bookend

Use three of the compound words above to fill in the blanks in the sentences below.

The band was playing _____

in the basement. They played as loud as they wanted

all night. This morning, I have a big

_____. If this keeps up, I'm going

to have a nervous _____!

COUNTDOWN: 10 - 9 - 8 - 7 - 6 - 5 - 4 - 3 - 2 - 1 - BLASTOFF!

9 **Fill in.** Complete the following sentences using the words constant and pressure.

If you hate talking in front of a group, speech class might cause you a lot of

_____.

Why? Because making speeches would give you

_____

stress.

◎ ◎ ◎ ◎ ◎ ◎ ◎ ◎ ◎ ◎ ◎ ◎ ◎

10 **Explain.** You have to participate in the school talent show. What's your act?

_____

_____

_____

_____

_____

Finish

Persuasive Paragraph | *Model*

Writing Focus
Persuasive Paragraph

A **persuasive paragraph** tries to convince the reader to share the writer's opinions.

▶ **Read Ashley's paragraph about stopping teen gossip.**

Student Model

> ### No More Gossip
> #### by Ashley Arroyo
>
> I strongly believe that the worst problem teens face is gossip. First of all, the Internet has made gossip worse than ever. People can post rumors on message boards without even leaving their own names. A second reason is that gossip can really hurt people. My friend Mike was arrested for shoplifting. His friend Derek told people, and now students make fun of Mike. The most important reason to stop gossip is that once a rumor starts, it's hard to stop it. People become convinced of things that just aren't true, only because everyone repeats them. In conclusion, it's my firmly held principle that gossip is wrong and must be stopped.

Parts of a Persuasive Paragraph

▶ **Find these parts of Ashley's persuasive paragraph.**

1. Underline the sentence that states the writer's **opinion**.
2. Check three **reasons** that support the opinion.
3. Put a box around the reason you think is **strongest**.
4. Circle the **linking words** that connect the ideas.
5. Put a star beside the sentence that **restates** the writer's opinion.

Brainstorm

▶ Read the writing prompt in the middle of the idea web. Then use the boxes to help you brainstorm your ideas.

Problems With Friendships

Problems in School

Writing Prompt:
What's the worst problem teens face? Write a persuasive paragraph about why it's a problem.

Problems With Self-Esteem

Problems Outside of School

Plan Your Paragraph

Writing Prompt: What's the worst problem teens face? Write a persuasive paragraph about why it's a problem.

▶ Use this chart to plan and organize your paragraph.

Word Choices

_____

_____

_____

_____

_____

Your Opinion
• *I strongly believe that . . .*
• *The worst problem . . .*
• *Many teens feel pressure to . . .*

Reason 1
• *First of all, . . .*
• *One reason is that . . .*
• *A good thing to remember . . .*

Reason 2
• *A second reason is that . . .*
• *In addition, . . .*
• *Another important point . . .*

Reason 3
• *The most important reason is that . . .*
• *The most important point . . .*
• *Finally, . . .*

Conclusion/Recommendation
• *In conclusion, . . .*
• *Overall, . . .*
• *It's important that . . .*

Write Your Paragraph

▶ **Use this writing frame to write a first draft of your paragraph.**

_____
(title)

I strongly believe that _____

_____

_____

_____

First of all, _____

_____

_____

_____

A second reason is that _____

_____

_____

_____

The most important reason is that _____

_____

_____

_____

In conclusion, _____

_____

_____

_____

_____

Revise

▶ **Rate your paragraph. Then have a writing partner rate it.**

Scoring Guide			
weak	okay	good	strong
1	2	3	4

1. Does the first sentence clearly state the writer's **opinion**?

| Self | 1 | 2 | 3 | 4 |
| Partner | 1 | 2 | 3 | 4 |

2. Is the opinion supported by several **reasons**?

| Self | 1 | 2 | 3 | 4 |
| Partner | 1 | 2 | 3 | 4 |

3. Are the reasons given **strong** and **convincing**?

| Self | 1 | 2 | 3 | 4 |
| Partner | 1 | 2 | 3 | 4 |

4. Do **linking words** connect the ideas?

| Self | 1 | 2 | 3 | 4 |
| Partner | 1 | 2 | 3 | 4 |

5. Does the concluding sentence **restate** the writer's opinion?

| Self | 1 | 2 | 3 | 4 |
| Partner | 1 | 2 | 3 | 4 |

▶ Now revise your paragraph to make it stronger.

Grammar USING IRREGULAR VERBS

Most past-tense verbs end in *–ed*. **Irregular verbs** do not.

- You must remember the different spellings of irregular past-tense verbs.
- The verb *to be* is a common irregular verb. Its **present-tense** forms are I am, you are, he/she is. Its past-tense forms are I was, you were, he was.

Example

Present-Tense Verb	Past-Tense Verb
I am sorry for my actions.	I was sorry for my actions.
Amy sends out cards for birthdays.	She sent one to me last week.
They usually eat lunch at noon.	Yesterday, they ate lunch early.

► **Circle the correct past-tense verb in each sentence below.**

1. Carlos once [(did) doed] mean things to get approval.

2. He even got [catched caught] participating in a hazing.

3. Carlos's parents [made maked] the decision to talk to his teachers.

4. The teachers [ared were] worried about him.

5. After they spoke with Carlos, he [was were] nicer to everyone.

6. Carlos [finded found] a way to improve his self-esteem.

► **Rewrite the sentences below using the past-tense form of the verb.**

7. Eric **fall** off the train and died.

_____

8. His girlfriend **tell** him not to climb outside the train.

_____

9. His uncle **says** that peer pressure caused Eric's death.

_____

10. The accident **make** many teens stop and think.

_____

Edit *Look at the sentences in your own draft on page 125. Do all sentences use correct verb forms? Fix the ones that don't.*

Mechanics USING COMMAS WITH INTRODUCTORY WORDS

A **comma** follows an opening word or phrase at the beginning of a sentence.

- *Yes, No, Next,* and *Later* are examples of opening words.
- *In addition* and *After a while* are examples of opening phrases.

Example

Correct	Incorrect
Next, Kim began helping others. After a while, she felt better.	Next Kim began helping others. After a while she felt better.

▶ **Find and correct five errors in this paragraph.**

Student Model

I think that teens shouldn't smoke. One reason is that cigarettes make you smell bad. Later the scent will stay on your clothes and hair. A second reason is that cigarettes damuge your health. Yes even walking up stairs can wear you out. The most important reason is that tobacco is deadly. My aunt losed her life to lung cancer last year. In conclusion, I am convenced that smoking is a really bad habit.

Check and Correct

- ☐ Circle two spelling errors and correct them.
- ☐ Underline one verb-tense error and correct it.
- ☐ Insert two missing commas.

 Edit *Look at the sentences in your own draft on page 125. Are opening phrases and words followed by commas? Fix the ones that aren't.*

Final Draft / Present

▶ **Write a final draft of your paragraph on paper or the computer. Check it again and correct any errors before you present it.**

Teen Counselor

Counselors help people deal with problems in their lives. Patricia Gonzales is a teen counselor. She works with teens on health issues, including body image, self-esteem, and peer pressure. "It's not an easy job," Patricia says, "but it's definitely worth it. Seeing teens learn and grow is what it's all about."

Name: Patricia Gonzales

Hometown: Hartford, Connecticut

Job: Youth and Family Health Counselor

Duties:
- offers guidance to teens
- is aware of their school, health, and safety concerns
- works with groups on peer pressure issues

Skills:
- identifying teens who have serious problems
- leading respectful group discussions
- problem-solving situations involving school or families

Similar Jobs:
- school counselor
- drug counselor

Pay: $22,000 to $35,000 per year

Education: Bachelor's or Master's Degrees

Patricia Gonzales stands in front of a mural painted by teens she works with. Below, she talks with a teen.

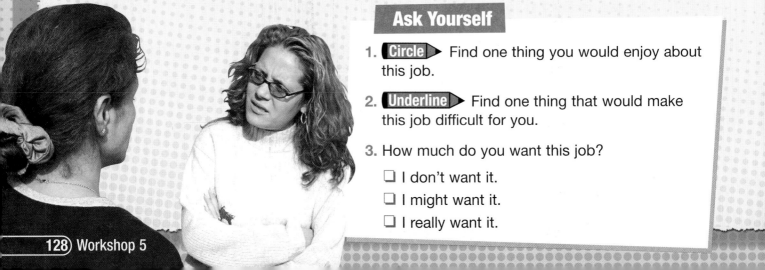

Ask Yourself

1. **Circle** Find one thing you would enjoy about this job.

2. **Underline** Find one thing that would make this job difficult for you.

3. How much do you want this job?

   ❑ I don't want it.

   ❑ I might want it.

   ❑ I really want it.

Evaluating a Teen-Targeted Ad

When Patricia Gonzales talks with teens about peer pressure and health issues, part of what they discuss is pressure from ads. An ad is designed to pressure you into buying something. Take a look at this ad. Be sure to read the fine print. Then answer the questions below.

LOSE WEIGHT NOW!

Lose up to 8 pounds **IN ONE WEEK!*** with Slimright!

Most people want to lose weight. Are you one of them? If so, our new all-natural Slimright pills will help the pounds melt away—for good. Take one pill every day, and you'll be surprised at **HOW MUCH** weight you will lose!

Plus, if you purchase a year's supply of 12 bottles, we'll give you an additional bottle of pills for FREE!** Start now! Call 1-800-555-5555 today to order!

Thin is in! Get thin fast with Slimright!

* Results not typical, based on trials that include exercise, diet, and nutrition counseling.

** A year's supply costs $300, with $15 shipping and handling added. A single bottle alone costs $75, with $15 for shipping and handling added.

▶ **Fill in the circle next to each correct answer.**

1. How much would it cost, total, for you to buy only one bottle of pills?

    Ⓐ $90
    Ⓑ It would be free.
    Ⓒ $300
    Ⓓ $315

2. Which phrase is a disclaimer (a statement that the company isn't responsible for something)?

    Ⓐ Call today!
    Ⓑ Results not typical.
    Ⓒ Lose weight now!
    Ⓓ Most people want to lose weight.

3. Why is the woman in the ad promoting the pills?

    Ⓐ She invented the pills.
    Ⓑ She was paid to appear in the ad.
    Ⓒ She thinks these pills work better than other weight-loss pills.
    Ⓓ She thinks these pills are the best bargain.

4. What will happen if someone takes these pills?

    Ⓐ They'll lose 7 pounds.
    Ⓑ They'll lose 8 pounds.
    Ⓒ It's impossible to tell.
    Ⓓ They'll gain weight.

5. Some ads have words in very fine print so that _____.

    Ⓐ you will save even more money
    Ⓑ you won't bother to read them
    Ⓒ you can exercise your eyes by reading them
    Ⓓ you will make the best shopping decision

Comprehension

▶ **Fill in the circle next to the correct answer.**

1. In Eric Alvarez's story, what is his main problem?
   - Ⓐ He fought with his aunt a lot.
   - Ⓑ He was scared of riding the subway.
   - Ⓒ He was pressured by his friends to do crazy stunts.
   - Ⓓ He had low self-esteem and was taking drugs.

2. Why are extreme diets and drugs *not* a solution to low self-esteem?
   - Ⓐ Extreme diets and drugs can damage your health.
   - Ⓑ You are either born with self-esteem, or you'll never have it.
   - Ⓒ Only doctors can help with low self-esteem.
   - Ⓓ Students who diet or use drugs are teased.

3. Peer pressure means _____.
   - Ⓐ the pressure you get from your parents
   - Ⓑ the pressure you get from your teachers
   - Ⓒ the pressure you get from people your own age
   - Ⓓ the pressure you get from a doctor

4. From the ages of 12 to 14, kids begin to rely more on _____.
   - Ⓐ their teachers
   - Ⓑ their friends
   - Ⓒ their families
   - Ⓓ authorities

5. Why do teens get involved in dangerous hazing?
   - Ⓐ They want to be better-looking.
   - Ⓑ They want to impress their parents and teachers.
   - Ⓒ The want to fit in with a group.
   - Ⓓ They want to stand out from the crowd.

Here's a tip.
You can answer some questions by looking directly in the text. For other questions, you have to combine what you already know with what you've read.

Vocabulary

▶ **Fill in the circle next to the correct definitions of the underlined words.**

1. <u>Authorities</u> say that good self-esteem helps teens deal with peer <u>pressure</u>.

   Ⓐ psychologists; happiness   Ⓒ teachers; project

   Ⓑ experts; force   Ⓓ parents; chore

2. Tianna <u>convinced</u> Rushawn to join her at the school dance, even though he was shy.

   Ⓐ invited along with other people   Ⓒ made someone believe or do something

   Ⓑ counted   Ⓓ allowed

3. After cheating to win the class election, Saria got a <u>negative</u> <u>image</u> at school.

   Ⓐ bad; the way others see you   Ⓒ unhappy; result

   Ⓑ happy; prize   Ⓓ total; victory

▶ **Fill in the circle next to the correct answer.**

4. Which two words are homophones?

   Ⓐ gum/gym   Ⓒ back/crack

   Ⓑ principal/principle   Ⓓ care/car

5. Which word is a compound word?

   Ⓐ picture   Ⓒ breakdown

   Ⓑ gigantic   Ⓓ computer

Short Answer

▶ **Use what you've read in this Workshop to answer the question below. Check your spelling and grammar.**

What is an example of peer pressure at your school?

_____

_____

_____

_____

WORKSHOP 6

LITERATURE

Comprehension Focus
Story Elements

READINGS
1 *The Fall of the House of Usher* >>Short Story
2 *from "The Haunted House"* >>Poetry

POE:

The Master of Horror

Meet the master of horror, Edgar Allan Poe. He lived from 1809 to 1849. His life was as mysterious as the stories he wrote. At age 40, Poe was found lying barely conscious in a street. Four days later he died, poor and almost unknown.

During his short, sad life, Poe wrote some of the scariest stories ever written. You are about to read one of them!

VOCABULARY BUILDER

◎ Target Word ▶ Read the Target Words. Rate each one using the scale below.*	Meaning ▶ Read the Target Word meanings. Write in the missing ones.	Example ▶ Finish the Target Word examples below. Write in the missing ones.
anxiety *anx•i•e•ty* *(noun)* ① ② ③		Snakes fill her with **anxiety**.
despair *de•spair* *(noun)* ① ② ③	a feeling of being very unhappy and having no hope	
peculiar *pe•cu•liar* *(adjective)* ① ② ③		I think it's peculiar when . . .
tremble *trem•ble* *(verb)* ① ② ③	to shake	
utter *ut•ter* *(verb)* ① ② ③		Words I might utter in fear are . . .

*Rating Scale

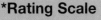

① = I don't know it at all.
② = I've seen it before.
③ = I know it and use it.

Comprehension Focus
Story Elements

A **short story** like "The Fall of the House of Usher" is a brief piece of fiction. To understand a short story, look for these elements:

1. **Setting** is where and when the story takes place. This story takes place in a strange old house a long time ago.

2. **Characters** are the people in the story.

Usher, a man who lives in an old house   **the narrator**, a friend of Usher's   **Madeline**, Usher's sister

3. **Plot** is the sequence of events in a story. The plot contains a problem that the main character needs to solve. In "The Fall of the House of Usher," the main character helps an old friend, Roderick Usher. But will he be able to handle Usher's illness—and his strange house?

▶ **Turn the page and start reading to find out what happens to the House of Usher.**

THE FALL OF THE HOUSE OF USHER

▶ **Fill in this chart as you reread the story.**

	Part 1 (pp. 136–137)	**Part 2** (pp. 138–141)	**Part 3** (pp. 142–143)
Setting	Time: *a gloomy autumn day* Place: *outside the old mansion*	Time: Place:	Time: Place:
Character	Who is the main character? Describe him/her:	How does the character change?	What is the character like now?
Plot Events	What happens at the beginning of the story?	What happens in the middle of the story?	How does the story end?

Active Reading

Star What does Usher ask the narrator to do?

VOCABULARY BUILDER

Target Word

depressing

de•press•ing *(adjective)*

Rate it: ① ② ③

Meaning

_____

_____

Example

_____

_____

_____

React

Write If you were Usher's friend, would you go to his house to help him? Why or why not?

_____

_____

_____

_____

The Fall of the House of Usher

adapted from the story by Edgar Allan Poe

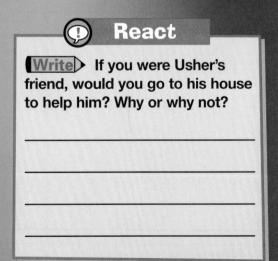

A letter arrived from my boyhood friend, Roderick Usher. He begged me to come visit him at his family house. Usher said that he was ill in both his body and mind. I could tell from his words that he was not well.

"You are my best and only friend," Usher wrote. "Perhaps you can ease my suffering by coming to stay with me a few weeks."

Usher's words disturbed me, because even though we had been companions since childhood, there was always a side of him I felt I didn't know. And I had heard many rumors about his strange family. Yet, as his friend, I felt obliged to obey his request.

I set out for Usher's house on a gloomy autumn day. As I came upon the ancient mansion, I sensed an atmosphere of decay. The stone walls of the house were crumbling, and the windows stared down at me like vacant eyes. Surrounding the house were dead bushes, rotting tree trunks, and a dark moat filled with

Words to Know! **vacant** empty

Story Elements

Setting

1. **Write** What word would you use to describe Usher's house?

_____

Character

2. **Underline** Find one detail that describes Usher. Find one detail that describes how the narrator is feeling.

Plot

3. **Write** What has happened in the story so far?

_____
_____
_____
_____
_____
_____
_____
_____
_____
_____

Now go to page 135. Add details to Part 1 of the chart.

sluggish water. My eyes fixed on a long crack that zigzagged down the front of the house like an open wound. The place was more than **depressing**—it was terrifying. A deep sense of despair crept over me.

The house had been in Usher's family for hundreds of years. The family was known for their artistic and musical talents, but there was something peculiar about them; not one member of the family ever moved out of the House of Usher. Generation after generation of Ushers had lived—and died—there.

Reluctantly, I urged my horse forward across the creaky bridge that spanned the moat. For a moment, I imagined that I was crossing into hell.

A servant gestured me inside the mansion, then led me down dark passages and up a staircase cloaked in shadows. Finally, I arrived at Usher's room.

Inside the room, the narrow, pointed windows were covered with blood-red draperies. The furniture was in tatters. Roderick Usher rose from a sofa to greet me. →

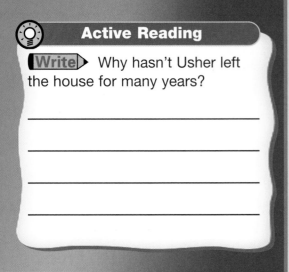

Active Reading

Write Why hasn't Usher left the house for many years?

_____

_____

_____

_____

VOCABULARY BUILDER

Target Word

mental

men•tal (adjective)

Rate it: ① ② ③

Meaning

_____

_____

Example

_____

_____

_____

 React

If you were the narrator and just saw Madeline, what would you think of her?

I couldn't believe my eyes as I gazed upon his face. My old friend was terribly altered from when I had last seen him. His eyes were watery and strangely enlarged, his lips seemed drained of color, his skin was as pale as a ghost's, and his hair floated wildly above his face.

Yet, when Usher greeted me, he reminded me of exactly how he had been as a boy. "So good to see you, friend. I'm very grateful that you came," Usher said. His words were warm and polite, yet his voice betrayed a nervous agitation.

Immediately, I asked him what the trouble was.

"I'm suffering from an evil family **mental** disease," he said. "I will perish from it, I know. My physicians say there is no cure." I asked him to describe the symptoms of the disease.

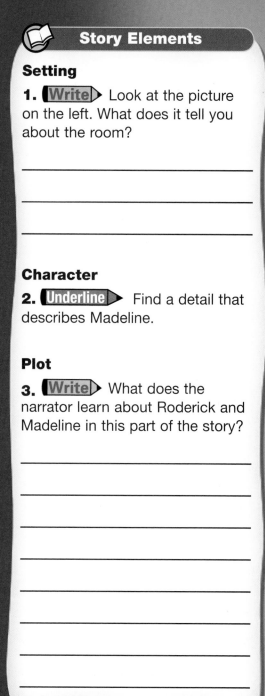

"I can barely eat," Usher said, "and I am fearful of straying away from the house. Sudden lights and noises disturb me. Everything, it seems, fills me with an overwhelming terror."

"What can I do to help you?" I asked.

"Sit, sit. Make yourself comfortable," said Usher. But comfort was not possible in that house. The sudden gusts of wind that blew through its shadowy walls sent a chill down my spine and through my heart.

Usher continued his story. He had not left the old mansion for many years because its gloom had influenced his mind, filling him with anxiety. Much of that anxiety was for his beloved sister, Madeline. She was his only living relative, but she too was afflicted by a peculiar disease.

"Her body and mind are wasting away," he explained. "If she died, I would be the last of the ancient race of Ushers."

As he spoke, I sensed a presence in the room. I glanced around and saw Madeline passing through the shadows. She disappeared into the darkness without speaking a word.

Usher buried his face in his hands and cried. "That will probably be the last time we see her alive," he said tragically. I decided not to mention her name again. This house—and its inhabitants—was beginning to play on my nerves.

For the next several days, I did everything in my power to lift Usher's spirits. We painted, read books, and I listened to him play melancholy music on his guitar. But never did we mention Madeline's name. ➡

Story Elements

Setting

1. **Write**▷ Look at the picture on the left. What does it tell you about the room?

_____

_____

_____

Character

2. **Underline**▷ Find a detail that describes Madeline.

Plot

3. **Write**▷ What does the narrator learn about Roderick and Madeline in this part of the story?

_____

_____

_____

_____

_____

_____

_____

Words to Know! **gusts** sudden, strong movements of wind

Active Reading

Star What do Usher and the narrator do after Madeline dies?

VOCABULARY BUILDER
Target Word

bizarre

bi•zarre *(adjective)*

Rate it: ① ② ③

Meaning

_____

_____

Example

_____

_____

_____

_____

React

What do you think is going on in the House of Usher?

_____

_____

_____

_____

For a while, I imagined that the gloom hanging over the House of Usher might lift, but I was wrong. Things were about to get much worse.

Usher's thoughts were growing more and more **bizarre**. One day he turned to me and asked, "Do you think the stone walls of this house are alive?"

I hesitated to answer, and stared at his wild eyes.

"They are alive," he said. "Look how each stone is arranged in the wall, like members of a family. These stones are alive indeed—unlike the lady Madeline, who is no more."

My heart froze, and I took a deep breath. Now Roderick Usher was the last of his family.

That evening, Usher asked me to help prepare his sister for burial in the family vault. Together, we laid her wasted-away body in an iron casket, then we carried the casket down to the vault which lay deep under the house in a shadowy dungeon. This dungeon was right below the bedroom where I was sleeping.

Words to Know! | **vault** an underground chamber

Story Elements

Setting

1. **Circle** ▸ Find where in the house the dungeon is.

Character

2. **Underline** ▸ What does Usher say about his relationship to Madeline?

Plot

3. **Write** ▸ What important event happens in this part of the story?

_____

_____

_____

_____

_____

_____

_____

_____

_____

Now go to page 135. Add details to Part 2 of the chart.

Before sliding the casket lid shut, I glanced at Madeline. There was a great resemblance to her brother. "We were twins," Usher whispered tragically.

I couldn't bear to look at this dead woman any longer. I was filled with emotion as we screwed tight the lid of the casket. Then we shut the iron door of the vault, which made a sharp grating sound as it closed.

After seven nights had passed, Usher's illness grew even worse. I would encounter him roaming about the house with no purpose, and he would sit slumped in his chair staring for hours at nothing.

On the eighth night, a violent storm began to gather, and I could not sleep. I began to tremble from a sense of horror I had never felt before. Then I heard a light step on the stairs. It was Usher, carrying a lantern.

"Have you not seen it?" he asked. His eyes looked half-insane. "Stay, stay, you will see it."

He flung open the window, and the fury of the storm burst in, nearly lifting us off our feet.

"Leave it closed!" I cried, and slammed the window shut.

Active Reading

Write ▶ What effect are the noises having on Usher?

_____

_____

_____

_____

VOCABULARY BUILDER
Target Word

remove

re•move (verb)

Rate it: ① ② ③

Meaning

_____

_____

Example

_____

_____

_____

⚡ React

Do you think the narrator did enough to help Usher? What would you have done?

Usher and I sat down, exhausted with emotion. I decided we should read a story out loud, to help calm us down. I began to read, but paused when I heard something rattle.

It's just the wind, I told myself. I continued to read.

Then I heard the peculiar rattle again, followed by a sharp, grating, screaming sound from below us—from the dungeon.

Usher was facing away from me. Did he hear what I was hearing? I attempted to continue reading, but the clanging and the screaming grew ever worse.

Completely unnerved, I leapt to my feet and rushed to my friend's chair. I tapped on his shoulder, and when he turned to me, I saw a sickly smile quivering on his lips.

"Yes, I hear it," he uttered. He almost seemed to be speaking to himself. "I hear it, and have heard it—for many long, long hours. Even for many days. Is she alive? Did we seal her in the casket while living? Oh, where will I escape? Is she coming? Are those her footsteps? Is that her heartbeat? Madman!"

Below us, a sharp, grating noise sounded as though a casket was **removing** itself from its place in the vault.

Usher cried out, "I don't know who is alive in this house and who is dead! Look, there she is!"

Suddenly, a strong gust of wind blew open the window and threw Usher to the floor. Outside, the figure of Madeline seemed to hover like a ghost. Then, with a low moan, the ghost of Madeline fell upon her brother and bore him to the floor—a corpse.

I fled that house in terror and panic. The storm had grown in intensity, and for an instant, the night flashed bright with lightning. I looked up and saw that the moon was blood-red. I ran across the bridge, and then looked back. At that moment, I saw the walls of the mansion split along the zigzag crack. Then, the dark waters of the moat swallowed up the stones of the HOUSE OF USHER. (END)

Words to Know! | quivering *shaking*

Story Elements

Setting

1. (Circle) ▷ Where are the noises coming from?

Character

2. (Underline) ▷ Find what Usher fears he has done to Madeline.

Plot

3. (Write) ▷ How does the story end?

_____

_____

_____

_____

_____

Now go to page 135. Complete Part 3 of the chart.

Skills Check

1. (Write) ▷ Tell what happens to Usher.

_____

_____

_____

_____

_____

2. (Star) ▷ Find how the narrator feels at the end of the story.

Active Reading

Star Where is the house located?

VOCABULARY BUILDER
Target Word

linger

lin•ger (verb)

Rate it: ① ② ③

Meaning

_____

_____

Example

_____

_____

_____

React

Write What kinds of things would make a house scary to you?

_____

_____

_____

_____

from **THE HAUNTED**

by **Jack Prelutsky**

On a hilltop bleak and bare
looms the castle of despair,
only phantoms **linger** there
within its dismal walls.
Through the dark they're creeping, crawling,
frenzied furies battling, brawling,
sprawling, calling, caterwauling
through the dusky halls.

Filmy visions, ever flocking,
dart through chambers, crudely mocking,
rudely rapping, tapping, knocking
on the crumbling doors.
Tortured spirits whine and wail,
they grope and grasp, they wildly flail,
their hollow voices rasp and rail
beneath the moldering floors.

In the corners, eyes are gleaming,
everywhere are nightmares streaming,
diabolic horrors screaming
in the sombrous air.
So shun this place where specters soar—
it's you and you they're waiting for
to haunt your souls forevermore
in their castle of despair.

Words to Know! **brawling** fighting in a noisy way

HOUSE

Literary Elements: Rhyme

Rhyme is two or more words that have ending syllables with the same sound.

Write Find the words that rhyme with:

bare: _____

wail: _____

gleaming: _____

_____

Literary Elements: Onomatopoeia

Onomatopoeia is the use of a word that sounds like the thing it stands for, such as *buzz* and *sizzle*.

Underline Find two examples of onomatopoeia in the poem.

TAKE THE WORD CHALLENGE

Start

1

Decide. How much would each of the following give you anxiety? Rate them.

1 = least anxiety
4 = most anxiety

_____ hearing a strange sound in the middle of the night

_____ riding on a killer roller coaster

_____ being locked in a room full of rats

_____ walking through a graveyard at midnight

2

Fill in. Finish these sentences about yourself.

Something that would make me _really, really_ tremble is

_____

I say this because

_____

_____

3

Synonyms

Synonyms are words that have similar meanings. Examples are _cold_ and _chilly_ and _tired_ and _sleepy._

Fill in. Match each word to its synonyms below.

> This movie is really **depressing**. I can't believe how **sad** it is.

peculiar   **nervousness**   **discard**

Synonym

remove, take away: _____

odd, strange: _____

worry, anxiety: _____

4

Decide. Which of the following uses of the word uttered are wrong—_really_ wrong?

☐ He uttered the ball to the pitcher.

☐ He uttered his name to the teacher.

☐ He uttered over the puddle.

☐ He uttered the whole song.

5

Tell. What's the most bizarre movie you have ever seen?

_____

_____

_____

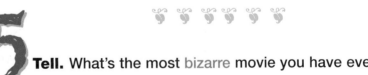

6

Tell about it. Finish this peculiar sentence.

I thought it was peculiar when the huge blue dog

_____

_____

_____

_____

7

Check it. Which are easy mental exercises for you?

❑ doing multiplication

❑ thinking of a funny joke

❑ remembering a phone number

❑ memorizing dates for a test

Coming up with great jokes is an easy **mental** exercise for me.

8

Okay. I know! I'm really **anxious** about this test. I'm feeling a lot of **anxiety**.

Word Families

A **word family** is a group of words that share the same base word and have related meanings, such as *terror, terrify,* and *terrorize. Terror* is a feeling of fear. *Terrify* and *terrorize* mean to make someone afraid.

Fill in. Complete the sentences with the correct form of the word *terror*.

1. I don't want to watch this movie. It will _____ me.

2. Don't _____ your little brother!

3. The _____ of the hurricane was finally over.

9

Check it. Which of the following would fill you with despair?

❑ a bad haircut

❑ a hard test

❑ having to remove a bandage

❑ having to eat vegetables

Don't **despair**. It will grow back.

10

Think about it. Finish the sentences.

I might linger in the school hallway if _____

_____

I might linger around the house if _____

_____

Finish

Writing Focus
Literature Review

A **literature review** presents the reviewer's opinion of a story.

▶ **Read Juanita's literature review of "Louisa, Please Come Home," the story in Workshop 3.**

Student Model

A Literature Review of "Louisa, Please Come Home"

by Juanita Morales

I thought "Louisa, Please Come Home" by Shirley Jackson was an excellent story. First of all, the author did a good job of showing Louisa's emotions. She gave many realistic clues about why Louisa was unhappy with her peculiar family. Another reason why I liked the story was that Louisa was able to disappear in a crowd. The author made it seem like this was really possible. Finally, I liked the story because of its twist ending. When Louisa went home, she was in for a surprise. I was not mentally prepared for what happened. In conclusion, I think this is a story that everybody would like to read.

Parts of a Literature Review
▶ **Find these parts of Juanita's literature review.**

1. Underline the sentence that clearly states the **writer's opinion** of the story.
2. Check three specific **reasons** that support the opinion.
3. Put a box around the reason you think is **strongest**.
4. Circle the **linking words** that connect the ideas.
5. Put a star by the sentence that **sums up** the writer's opinion.

Brainstorm

▶ Read the writing prompt in the middle of the idea web. Then use the boxes to help you brainstorm your ideas.

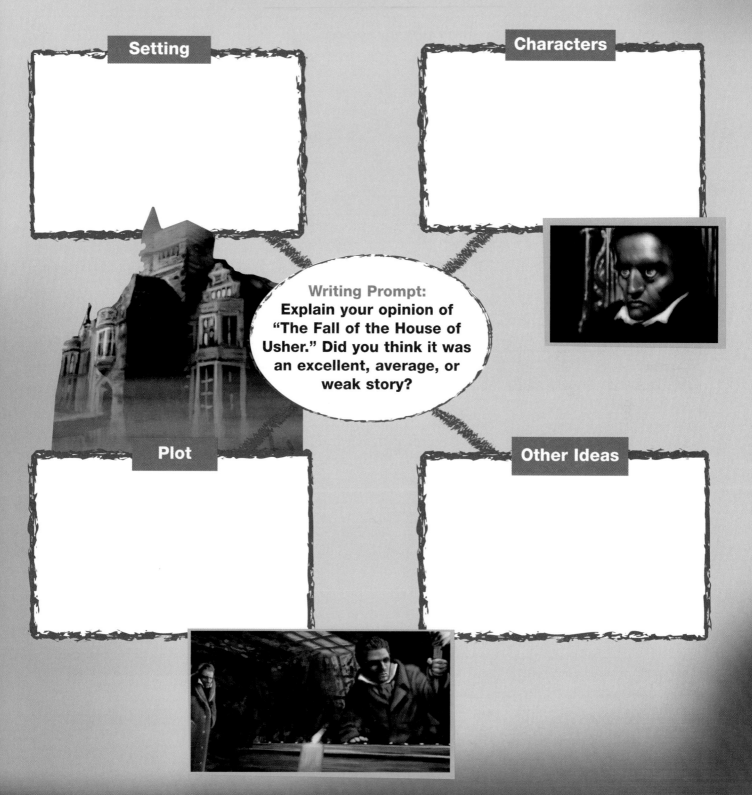

Setting

Characters

Writing Prompt:
Explain your opinion of "The Fall of the House of Usher." Did you think it was an excellent, average, or weak story?

Plot

Other Ideas

Plan Your Paragraph

Writing Prompt: Explain your opinion of "The Fall of the House of Usher." Did you think it was an excellent, average, or weak story?

▶ Use this chart to plan and organize your paragraph.

Word Choices

_____

_____

_____

_____

_____

Statement About the Story

• I thought . . .

• The story . . .

• In my opinion, . . .

Example or Reason 1

• First of all, . . .

• The first reason . . .

• To start with, . . .

Example or Reason 2

• Another reason . . .

• Secondly, . . .

• Also, . . .

Example or Reason 3

• Finally, . . .

• The third reason . . .

• In addition, . . .

Concluding Statement

• In conclusion, . . .

• I recommend . . .

• I do not recommend . . .

Write Your Paragraph

▶ Use this writing frame to write a first draft of your paragraph.

_____
(title)

I thought _____
_____
_____
_____

First of all, _____
_____
_____
_____

Another reason _____
_____
_____
_____

Finally, _____
_____
_____
_____

In conclusion, _____
_____
_____
_____
_____

Revise

▶ Rate your paragraph. Then have a writing partner rate it.

Scoring Guide			
weak	okay	good	strong
1	2	3	4

1. Does the beginning clearly state the **writer's opinion** of the story?

Self	1	2	3	4
Partner	1	2	3	4

2. Are there specific **reasons** that support the opinion?

Self	1	2	3	4
Partner	1	2	3	4

3. Are the reasons given **strong and convincing**?

Self	1	2	3	4
Partner	1	2	3	4

4. Do **linking words** connect the ideas?

Self	1	2	3	4
Partner	1	2	3	4

5. Does the ending **sum up** the writer's opinion?

Self	1	2	3	4
Partner	1	2	3	4

▶ Now revise your paragraph to make it stronger.

Grammar SUBJECT-VERB AGREEMENT

The **subject and verb** in a sentence must agree in number.

- A singular verb tells what one person, place, or thing is doing. It usually ends in *-s* or *-es*.
- A plural verb tells what more than one person, place, or thing is doing. It usually does not end in *-s* or *-es*.

Example

Singular Subject and Verb	Plural Subject and Verb
A noise comes from below.	The noises come from below.
Usher closes the door to the vault.	We close the door to the vault.

▶ **Put an X next to the sentences that have subject-verb agreement errors.**

1. The man enter a dimly lit room.   ___X___

2. Usher suffers from an evil disease.   _____

3. Usher and his sister looks very ill.   _____

4. She disappear into the darkness.   _____

5. They slide the casket into the empty vault.   _____

6. The guest tremble with fear.   _____

▶ **Rewrite the following sentences with correct subject-verb agreement. (Be sure to keep all the sentences in present tense.)**

7. A gust of wind throw Usher to the floor!

_____

8. The casket scrape against the stone floor.

_____

9. The walls of the house crumbles to the ground.

_____

10. Usher and his family disappears forever.

_____

Edit ▶ *Take a close look at each of the sentences in your draft on page 151. Do the subjects and verbs all agree? If not, fix them.*

Mechanics USING POSSESSIVES

A **possessive noun** shows ownership.

- Add an apostrophe (') and an -s to a singular noun.
- Add an apostrophe to a plural noun that ends in -s.

Example

Correct	Incorrect
Poe's story scared me. The friends' voices were low.	Poes story scared me. The friends voices were low.

▶ **Find and correct five errors in this paragraph.**

Student Model

> I didn't like the story "Louisa, Please Come Home." First, I thought Louisa might feel anxiuty. But she shows no emotion about leaving her family. Next, she disappear into a big city. But I doubt that she'd get away so easily. Then, Louisas family doesn't recognize her later. I can't understand how that would happen. I don't think anybody would believe Jacksons bizarr story.

Check and Correct

- ☐ Circle two spelling errors and correct them.
- ☐ Underline two errors with possessives and correct them.
- ☐ Correct one subject-verb agreement error.

Edit ➔ *Look at the sentences in your draft on page 151. Are all the possessive nouns formed correctly? If not, fix them.*

Final Draft /Present

▶ **Write a final draft of your paragraph on paper or the computer. Check it again and correct any errors before you present it.**

Edgar Allan Poe

Edgar Allan Poe didn't just write horror stories, he also wrote some beautiful poems. In addition, he invented the modern detective story.

Poe's life was as strange as his stories. He was born in 1809 in Boston, Massachusetts. After a very difficult childhood, he spent some time in college and the army. But it was always his dream to become a poet.

Poe found jobs as a writer and editor. However, he was quickly fired because of his wild behavior. At the age of 18, Poe's first piece of writing was published. Still, his life remained a struggle. At age 40, Poe was found lying in a Baltimore street. He was barely conscious. How did he get there? It is still a mystery. Four days later, Poe died. At the time, he was poor and almost unknown. Today Poe is regarded as one of the greatest American writers of all time.

Famous Stories:

"The Murders in the Rue Morgue"
"The Pit and the Pendulum"
"The Tell-Tale Heart"

> "I wish I could write as mysterious as a cat."

Ask Yourself

1. **Underline** ▶ How old was Poe when he was first published?

2. **Circle** ▶ Which of Poe's stories sounds the most interesting?

3. How much do you want to be a writer?

   ❑ I don't want it.

   ❑ I might want it.

   ❑ I really want it.

Selecting a DVD

Looking for a good movie? You might check out the DVD section of your video store. DVD covers carry a lot of information about the movie inside. Take a look at this DVD cover.

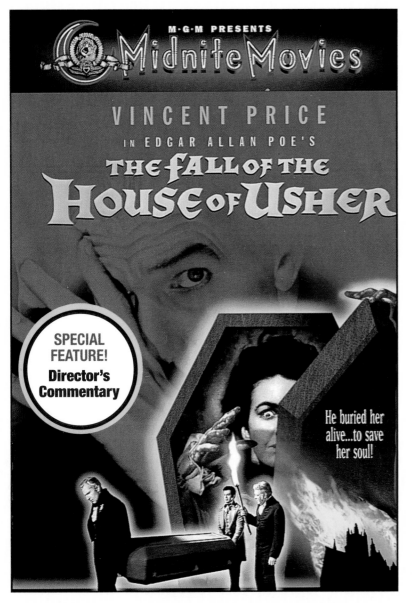

▶ **Fill in the circle next to each correct answer.**

1. What movie is inside this DVD case?
   - Ⓐ "Midnite Movies"
   - Ⓑ "The Fall of the House of Usher"
   - Ⓒ "Vincent Price"
   - Ⓓ "Buried Alive"

2. Who stars in the movie?
   - Ⓐ MGM
   - Ⓑ Edgar Allan Poe
   - Ⓒ Vincent Price
   - Ⓓ Usher

3. What special feature is included on this DVD?
   - Ⓐ the director's commentary
   - Ⓑ a free sticker
   - Ⓒ a CD of the soundtrack
   - Ⓓ No special features are included.

4. Based on the DVD cover, what kind of movie is this likely to be?
   - Ⓐ an action movie
   - Ⓑ a romantic comedy
   - Ⓒ a mystery
   - Ⓓ a horror movie

5. Why would you read a DVD cover?
   - Ⓐ to see how the movie will end
   - Ⓑ to decide whether or not to watch it
   - Ⓒ to learn why it was unsuccessful
   - Ⓓ to find out how to return it

Comprehension

▶ **Fill in the circle next to the correct answer.**

1. Where does "The Fall of the House of Usher" take place?

Ⓐ Poe's house

Ⓑ Madeline's backyard

Ⓒ Usher's house

Ⓓ the narrator's living room

2. Based on this story, you can tell that Madeline _____.

Ⓐ was in love with the narrator

Ⓑ had been sick for a long time

Ⓒ loved her family's home

Ⓓ didn't get along with Usher

> **Here's a tip.**
> Some short-answer questions ask for your opinion. Be sure to back up your thoughts with text evidence.

3. What happens to Usher's house after the narrator leaves?

Ⓐ It becomes haunted.

Ⓑ It sinks into the water.

Ⓒ It is sold.

Ⓓ It is turned into a museum.

4. Which pair of words best describes the narrator?

Ⓐ slow and clumsy

Ⓑ funny and irresponsible

Ⓒ cruel and selfish

Ⓓ concerned and thoughtful

5. How are the story and the poem similar?

Ⓐ Both are by Edgar Allan Poe.

Ⓑ Both are set in modern times.

Ⓒ Both have a mood of anxiety and terror.

Ⓓ Both have main characters who help a friend.

Vocabulary

▶ **Fill in the circle next to the correct definition of the underlined word.**

1. The sound from the dungeon made the narrator <u>tremble</u>.

Ⓐ shake   Ⓒ quick

Ⓑ laugh   Ⓓ angry

2. When Usher's sister died, he was filled with <u>despair</u>.

Ⓐ hopefulness   Ⓒ great unhappiness

Ⓑ lack of feeling   Ⓓ chills

3. "I hear the noises," Usher <u>uttered</u>.

Ⓐ imagined   Ⓒ laughed

Ⓑ wrote   Ⓓ said

▶ **Choose the correct synonym for the underlined word.**

4. Usher's house was very <u>peculiar</u>.

Ⓐ dark   Ⓒ old

Ⓑ strange   Ⓓ gloomy

▶ **Choose the correct word to fill in the blank.**

5. This story gave me a feeling of _____.

Ⓐ anxiously   Ⓒ anxiety

Ⓑ angry   Ⓓ anxious

Short Answer

▶ **Use what you've read in this Workshop to answer the question below. Check your spelling and grammar.**

Why do you think Poe is called the "Master of Horror"?

_____

_____

_____

_____

WORKSHOP 7

NONFICTION

Comprehension Focus
Cause and Effect

READINGS
1 *Freaky Fish Invasion* >> Newspaper Article
2 *Island of Snakes* >> Magazine Article
3 *America's Least Wanted* >> Science Text

Alien INVADERS

Help! The aliens have invaded!

But these aliens don't come from outer space. They're plants and animals from other countries. When they land in the U.S., alien invaders cause huge problems. They destroy the environment. They kill native plants and animals. They even threaten people.

Scientists know these invaders must be stopped. The question is: How?

VOCABULARY BUILDER

◎ Target Word ▶ Read the Target Words. Rate each one using the scale below.*	Meaning ▶ Read the Target Word meanings. Write in the missing ones.	Example ▶ Finish the Target Word examples below. Write in the missing ones.
alter al•ter (verb) ① ② ③		*If I could alter my school, I would . . .*
environment en•vi•ron•ment (noun) ① ② ③	*surroundings or habitat*	
invade in•vade (verb) ① ② ③		*If _____ invaded my town, I would . . .*
method meth•od (noun) ① ② ③	*a way of doing something*	
species spe•cies (noun) ① ② ③		 We're different **species**, but we can still get along.

*Rating Scale

①= I don't know it at all.
②= I've seen it before.
③= I know it and use it.

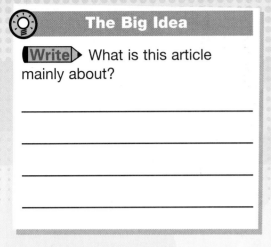

The Big Idea

Write What is this article mainly about?

_____

_____

_____

_____

VOCABULARY BUILDER
Target Word

poisonous

poi•son•ous (adjective)

Rate it: ① ② ③

Meaning

_____

_____

Example

_____

_____

_____

React

Do you think it's right for scientists to kill invader species? Why or why not?

The Chinese snakehead fish is an invader species.

Freaky Fish Invasion
Scientists Stalk the Snakehead Fish

September 4, 2002— Last week, top scientists rushed to a small pond in Maryland. The pond had been invaded by some very strange fish. And the fish were causing major problems!

The freaky fish were northern snakeheads from China. Snakehead fish are three feet long and slimy. Their skin is covered with black spots.

How did these alien invaders get here? They were brought into the U.S. illegally. Then someone dumped them into the Maryland pond.

Snakeheads have big mouths and sharp teeth. They are very powerful predators. So, the other fish didn't have a chance. The snakeheads ate them up.

The scientists had another thing to worry about. The Little Patuxent River is near the pond. Because snakeheads can crawl short distances across land, they might reach the river. They'd kill the fish there, too.

To stop the snakeheads, police sprayed **poisonous** chemicals into the water. As a result, the snakeheads died. Then scientists filled the pond with native fish. The pond is safe—until the next invader arrives. **END**

Words to Know! **native** originally from an area

Cause and Effect

A **cause** is the reason something happens. An **effect** is the result of a cause.
To find the cause and effect:

- Ask yourself "Why did it happen?" to find the cause.

- Ask yourself "What happened?" to find the effect.

- Look for signal words or phrases such as *because, so, as a result, therefore,* and *for this reason.*

▶ **Fill in this chart with the cause-and-effect relationships in "Freaky Fish Invasion."**

Cause

_____
_____
_____
_____
_____

Effect

So, the other fish didn't have a chance. The snakeheads ate them up.
_____
_____

Cause

_____
_____
_____
_____
_____
_____
_____

Effect

_____
_____
_____
_____
_____
_____
_____

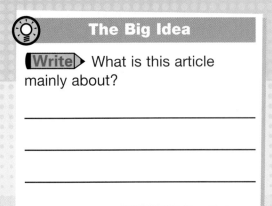

The Big Idea

Write ▷ What is this article mainly about?

_____

_____

_____

VOCABULARY BUILDER
Target Word

interfere

in•ter•fere (verb)

Rate it: ① ② ③

Meaning

_____

_____

Example

_____

_____

_____

 React

What do you think Guam should do about the brown tree snake?

Island of Snakes

Fifty years ago, the brown tree snake arrived in Guam. Life hasn't been the same since.

If you visit the island of Guam, watch out for snakes. They hang from the trees. They hide in the bushes. They might even slither into your bed while you're sleeping!

Snakes Take Over

Guam is a tiny island in the middle of the Pacific Ocean. Brown tree snakes arrived here from New Guinea, another island. Nobody meant to bring the snakes to Guam. They crawled onto military planes and ships by accident. Then they slithered off onto the island. When they did, everything changed.

Brown tree snakes are an alien species to the island. Because they have no natural predators on Guam, the snakes keep multiplying. In fact, they're completely out of control. Currently, there are more than 13,000

Above, the brown tree snake hangs from a tree in Guam. At right, a woman holds a full-grown brown tree snake.

snakes per square mile on the island.

Dangerous Damage

Since invading Guam, the brown tree snakes have damaged the island's environment. They've killed and eaten native lizards, birds, and small mammals. As a result, 12 species of birds are now extinct. The brown tree snakes ate them all!

The snakes **interfere** with life on Guam in other ways. They like to hang out on power lines. Because they weigh so much, the power lines snap. Since 1978, they've caused more than 1,200 power outages. For this reason, the lights go out regularly. Refrigerators break down. Computer screens go blank. It costs a lot to fix the damage caused by the snakes. ➡

Words to Know! | **multiply** to grow in number rapidly

1. **Write** ▷ Find the cause that tells you why the brown tree snakes multiplied so fast in "Snakes Take Over."

_____

_____

_____

_____

_____

_____

_____

2. **Underline** ▷ Find signal words or phrases in "Dangerous Damage."

3. **Write** ▷ What are two effects of the power outages in "Dangerous Damage"?

•_____

_____

_____

_____

_____

_____

•_____

_____

_____

_____

_____

Active Reading

Circle ▶ What does a brown tree snake bite feel like?

VOCABULARY BUILDER
Target Word

release

re•lease (verb)

Rate it: ① ② ③

Meaning

_____

_____

Example

_____

_____

_____

React

Write ▶ Which animal is worse—the brown tree snake or the snakehead fish? Why?

_____

_____

_____

_____

_____

_____

People vs. Snakes

The brown tree snakes also threaten people. They crawl into houses. They creep inside schools. What are they looking for? Food!

The snakes don't eat people, but they *do* bite. What happens when a brown tree snake bites you? You will be in pain, but you won't die. The venom is only mildly poisonous. The bite feels like a very bad bee sting.

The snakes are more dangerous for children. Children can't fight off a snake as well. Because the snake can get a better grip around a small victim, its bite **releases** more venom. The venom is so powerful that some children have trouble breathing after a brown tree snake bite.

Endless Battle

Brown tree snakes have altered Guam forever. Now, scientists fear the snakes might invade other

Brown tree snakes are collected in Guam—and destroyed.

> **The snakes don't eat people, but they *do* bite.**

islands, too. The same phenomenon that happened in Guam could happen in other countries. The snakes might become an international problem.

Some time ago, brown tree snakes were found at an airport in Hawaii. Scientists knew they had to stop the snakes before they caused a disaster. Therefore, they killed the snakes right away.

The battle with the brown tree snake goes on. In the end, everyone hopes that the scientists will win. **END**

Words to Know! **phenomenon** an event of scientific interest

Comprehension Focus
Cause and Effect

▶ Fill in this chart with the cause-and-effect relationships in "People vs. Snakes" and "Endless Battle."

Cause

_____

_____

_____

_____

Effect

_____

_____

_____

_____

Cause

_____

_____

_____

_____

Effect

_____

_____

_____

_____

Cause

_____

_____

_____

_____

Effect

_____

_____

_____

_____

The Big Idea

Write What is this article mainly about?

_____

_____

_____

VOCABULARY BUILDER

Target Word

responsible

re•spon•si•ble *(adjective)*

Rate it:

Meaning

_____

_____

Example

_____

_____

_____

 React

If someone planted a kudzu bush in a park near your home, what would you do?

AMERICA'S LEAST WANTED

KUDZU

RED FIRE ANTS

ZEBRA MUSSELS

NORTHERN SNAKEHEAD

Some animals and plants are bad for America. Find out the scary, gross facts about these alien invaders.

The Least-Wanted List

Did you know that the U.S. has a "Least-Wanted List"? It's true. But unlike the "Most-Wanted List," this isn't a list of people. It's a list of plants and animals. They have names like the Mexican fruit fly, the giant African snail, and the Asian longhorn beetle. Why are these creatures on the list? They're invader species.

Invader species are nonnative plants or animals that come from other countries. When they invade, they cause major damage. They can damage the environment, native plants and animals, and even the economy.

Attack of the Vines

One invader species is creeping all over the southern U.S. It's called kudzu. Kudzu is a vine brought here from Asia. At first, farmers used it to keep their land healthy. But soon, kudzu grew out of control. Because kudzu thrives in the warm climate of the South, it now covers seven million acres of land. It's not stopping, either. Kudzu can grow up to one foot a day. A single root can weigh 400 pounds!

Kudzu is **responsible** for destroying native forests. It climbs all over trees and blocks out the sunlight. As a result, the trees die. Kudzu can also wrap itself around a car. It can even blanket a house! People used to joke that kudzu might even creep into their windows at night and strangle them! Now kudzu is creeping into cities all over the U.S. ➡

| Words to Know! | **climate** weather conditions |

Cause and Effect

1. **Underline** ▷ Find three effects of invader species in "The Least-Wanted List."

2. **Write** ▷ In "Attack of the Vines," what caused kudzu to spread over seven million acres?

_____

_____

_____

_____

_____

Review: Problem and Solution

1. **Underline** ▷ What problem is discussed in "Attack of the Vines?"

2. **Write** ▷ How do you think people might attempt to solve the problem?

_____

_____

_____

_____

_____

_____

Active Reading

Circle What invader species is invading the food chain in the Great Lakes?

VOCABULARY BUILDER

Target Word

capable

ca•pa•ble (adjective)

Rate it:

Meaning

_____

_____

Example

_____

_____

_____

React

Write Most people don't know about invader species. How should scientists get the word out?

_____

_____

_____

_____

_____

 TEXT FEATURE **Reading a Flowchart**

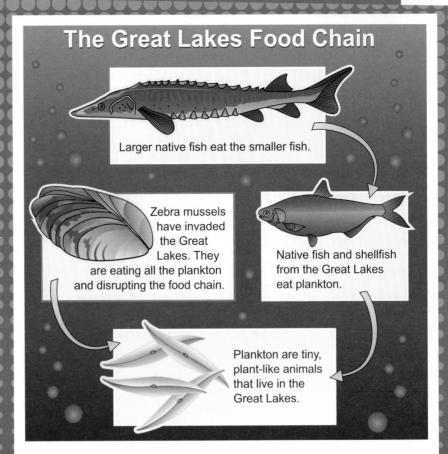

The Great Lakes Food Chain

Larger native fish eat the smaller fish.

Zebra mussels have invaded the Great Lakes. They are eating all the plankton and disrupting the food chain.

Native fish and shellfish from the Great Lakes eat plankton.

Plankton are tiny, plant-like animals that live in the Great Lakes.

A flowchart shows how the parts of a process are connected.

1. According to this chart, where are plankton on the food chain?

   Ⓐ at the top   Ⓑ at the bottom

   Ⓒ in the middle   Ⓒ they're not in the food chain

2. How are zebra mussels disrupting the food chain?

   _____

   _____

3. What do large native fish typically eat?

   _____

   _____

A Threat to the Food Chain

In the Great Lakes, one invader species is destroying nature's food chain. A food chain links different plants and animals together. Each species is food for the next one on the chain. If one plant or animal in the chain is destroyed, it affects the entire food chain.

Zebra mussels are harming the native food chain in the Great Lakes. The mussels came from Russia in 1988. They are eating the plankton in the lakes—food other fish depend on. So, the entire food chain is in danger.

A Deadly Sting

Some invader species are killers. In the 1930s, red fire ants crossed the Mexican border into the U.S. Before long, they were responsible for the deaths of thousands of animals. The ants attack an animal by crawling into its eyes and nose. Then they sting—all at once. The stings are deadly enough to kill a large animal like a deer.

The U.S. government has methods for monitoring invasive species and stopping them. Field workers fight the invaders with poison, explosives, and electric shock. But we aren't **capable** of controlling every invader, because too many alien species are in too many places. So be on the look-out yourself—for America's Least Wanted! END

Words to Know!	**monitoring** tracking or following

Red fire ants devour a baby bird.

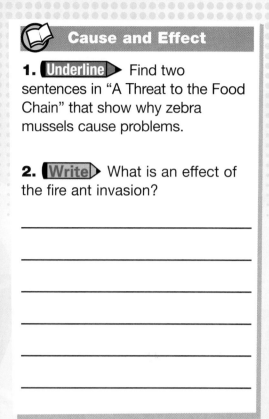

Cause and Effect

1. Underline ▷ Find two sentences in "A Threat to the Food Chain" that show why zebra mussels cause problems.

2. Write ▷ What is an effect of the fire ant invasion?

_____

_____

_____

_____

_____

_____

Skills Check

1. Underline ▷ How are field workers fighting invader species?

2. Write ▷ Why can't we stop invader species?

_____

_____

_____

_____

_____

_____

TAKE THE WORD CHALLENGE

Start

1 **Check them.** Which of the following things are you capable of?

☐ running a mile in 10 minutes

☐ drawing a realistic picture of a friend

☐ dancing like someone from a music video

☐ making three baskets in a row in basketball

2 **Decide.** If you caught a poisonous bug, would you kill it, keep it as a pet, or release it outside?

What do you do with it?

_____

Tell why. _____

_____

_____

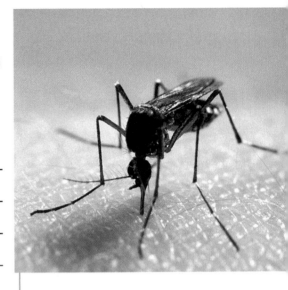

Some say this trick is hard, but for me, it's a **piece of cake**!

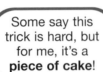

3 **Idioms**

An **idiom** is an expression that means something different from the separate words. Something interesting can be called "food for thought." Something that is easy to do is "a piece of cake."

Match these idioms to their meanings.

"You'll knock their socks off!"   You might get into trouble.

"You're flirting with disaster!"   You'll impress them.

Now, finish these sentences:

I'll knock your socks off with my _____

_____

It would be flirting with disaster if I _____

_____

4 **Decide.** The school has asked your advice about the school lunch menu. How would you alter it?

I would remove:

_____

I would add:

_____

5 **Check.** Which species would win in a "Battle of the Species"? Pick one in each row.

☐ rat   vs.   ☐ porcupine

☐ shark   vs.   ☐ octopus

☐ snake   vs.   ☐ hawk

6 **Check them.** Which of the following **environments** would you prefer to live in?

- ❑ a hot, humid one
- ❑ a cold, snowy one
- ❑ a wet, windy one
- ❑ a dry, dusty one

7 **Check them.** Which of these are you **responsible** enough to handle?

- ❑ baby-sitting a 1-year-old
- ❑ being captain of a team
- ❑ cooking a meal for your family
- ❑ taking a celebrity on a tour of your school

9 **Think about it.** Which two are the worst?

- ❑ invading a friend's email account
- ❑ invading a friend's privacy by listening in on his or her phone calls
- ❑ invading a friend's privacy by reading his or her journal
- ❑ invading a friend's privacy by going through his or her locker

8 **Using a Dictionary**

Look in the dictionary when you're not sure how to pronounce a word. A dictionary will tell you how to say it with a pronunciation guide. Check out the pronunciation of *species* and *specimen* below. They look like they might be pronounced alike, but they aren't.

Look up the pronunciation of these tricky words in the glossary. Say them to a partner. Give yourself a check when you pronounce each word correctly:

_____ agony

_____ assure

_____ luxury

_____ quiver

_____ vault

> **spe·cies** (spee-sheez *or* spee-seez) *noun* One of the groups into which animals and plants of the same genus are divided according to their shared characteristics.

> **spec·i·men** (spess-uh-muhn) *noun* A sample, or an example used to stand for a whole group, as in *a butterfly specimen* or *a blood specimen*.

10 **Choose.** Your parents **interfere** in your social life. What's the best **method** for getting them to back off?

- ❑ introduce them to your friends
- ❑ let them listen in on your phone calls
- ❑ tell them exactly where you are and what time you'll be home

Other: _____

_____

Finish

Writing Focus

Persuasive Paragraph

A persuasive paragraph tries to convince the reader to share the writer's opinions.

▶ **Read Alex's persuasive paragraph about keeping tarantulas as pets.**

Student Model

Stop Pet Tarantulas Now!

By Alex Garcia

I strongly believe that tarantulas should not be allowed as pets. One reason is that tarantulas can be poisonous. If a tarantula was released from its cage, it could be responsible for hurting people. A second reason is that it's hard to take care of a tarantula. A tarantula owner is probably not really capable of caring for this kind of pet. Most importantly, if a pregnant tarantula got loose, it could alter a whole environment. Who wants to see baby tarantulas crawling around their neighborhood? Not me! For these reasons, I believe that tarantulas should be outlawed as pets.

Parts of a Persuasive Paragraph

▶ **Find these parts of Alex's persuasive paragraph.**

1. Underline the sentence that states the writer's **opinion**.
2. Check three **reasons** that support the opinion.
3. Put a box around the reason you think is **strongest**.
4. Circle the **linking words** that connect the ideas.
5. Put a star beside the sentence that **restates** the writer's opinion.

Brainstorm

▶ Read the writing prompt in the middle of the idea web. Then use the boxes to help you brainstorm your ideas.

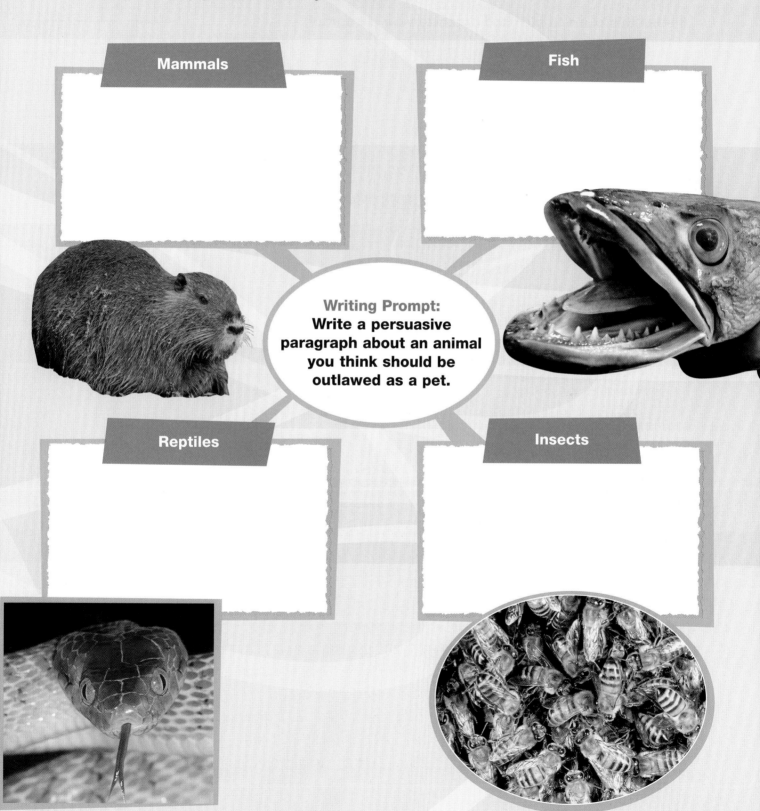

Mammals

Fish

Writing Prompt:
Write a persuasive paragraph about an animal you think should be outlawed as a pet.

Reptiles

Insects

Plan Your Paragraph

Writing Prompt: Write a persuasive paragraph about an animal you think should be outlawed as a pet.

▶ **Use this chart to plan and organize your paragraph.**

Word Choices

_____

_____

_____

_____

_____

Topic/Opinion Sentence

• *I strongly believe that . . .*

• *Some animals are . . .*

• *A pet is (not) a . . .*

Reason 1

• *One reason is that . . .*

• *First of all, . . .*

• *The worst thing . . .*

Reason 2

• *A second reason is that . . .*

• *In addition, . . .*

• *Another reason . . .*

Reason 3

• *Most importantly, . . .*

• *Finally, . . .*

• *It's also important to remember . . .*

Conclusion

• *For these reasons, . . .*

• *In conclusion, . . .*

• *The best way . . .*

Write Your Paragraph

▶ Use this writing frame to write a first draft of your paragraph.

_____
(title)

I strongly believe that _____

_____

_____

One reason is that _____

_____

_____

A second reason is that _____

_____

_____

Most importantly, _____

_____

_____

For these reasons, _____

_____

_____

Revise

▶ **Rate your paragraph. Then have a writing partner rate it.**

Scoring Guide			
weak	okay	good	strong
1	2	3	4

1. Does the first sentence clearly state the writer's **opinion**?

Self	1	2	3	4
Partner	1	2	3	4

2. Is the opinion supported by several **reasons**?

Self	1	2	3	4
Partner	1	2	3	4

3. Are the reasons given **strong and convincing**?

Self	1	2	3	4
Partner	1	2	3	4

4. Do **linking words** connect the reasons?

Self	1	2	3	4
Partner	1	2	3	4

5. Does the concluding sentence **restate** the writer's opinion?

Self	1	2	3	4
Partner	1	2	3	4

▶ Now revise your paragraph to make it stronger.

Grammar USING SUBJECT AND OBJECT PRONOUNS

A **pronoun** is a word that takes the place of a noun in a sentence.

- Use a **subject pronoun** in the subject of a sentence.
- Use an **object pronoun** after a verb or after a word such as *for* or *to*.

Example

Subject Pronoun	Object Pronoun
I never liked snakes.	Snakes have always scared me.
We want to leave the island.	Snakes are too gross for us.
She found two in the house.	One snake almost bit her.
They are just creepy.	My sister and I hate them.

▶ **Circle the correct pronoun. Write whether it is a subject or object pronoun.**

1. The snakehead fish tried to bite [he (him)]. *object*

2. [He Him] showed the fish to his parents. _____

3. [They Them] called the game warden. _____

4. The game warden took the fish away with [her she]. _____

5. Roberto has a photo of all of [them they] with the fish. _____

6. [I Me] don't want to catch a snakehead fish. _____

▶ **Rewrite these sentences using a pronoun for the underlined words.**

7. <u>My grandmother</u> said that ants have taken over her yard.

   _____

8. She sprayed her rose garden to stop <u>the invader ants</u>.

   _____

9. My sister helped <u>Grandma</u> cut down the kudzu.

   _____

10. <u>My cousins</u> helped out in the yard, too.

    _____

 Edit *Take a close look at each of the sentences in your draft on page 175. Do they all use subject and object pronouns correctly? Fix the ones that don't.*

Usage AVOIDING DOUBLE NEGATIVES

Negatives are words that express *no* or *not*.

- Use only one negative word to express a single negative idea.
- It is incorrect to use two negatives to express a negative idea.

| Example | |
Correct	Incorrect
Tigers should never be pets. The snake didn't eat anything.	Tigers shouldn't never be pets. The snake didn't eat nothing.

▶ **Find and correct five errors in this paragraph.**

Check and Correct
☐ Circle two spelling errors and correct them.
☐ Underline one subject-object pronoun error and correct it.
☐ Correct two double-negative errors.

Student Model

I think that pit bulls shouldn't be allowed as pets. One reason is that these dogs were bred to fight. Them are capuble of fighting to the death. A second reason is sometimes they attack without no warning. Pit bulls won't never let go once they bite. The most important reason is that sevral people have been killed by pit bulls recently. Obviously, this animal should not be allowed as a pet.

 Edit Look at the sentences in your own draft on page 175. Are they free of double negatives? Fix the ones that have double negatives.

Final Draft/Present

▶ **Write a final draft of your paragraph on paper or on the computer. Check it again and correct any errors before you present it.**

Careers

Wild Animal Keeper

Lisette Ramos is a wild animal keeper. She cares for reptiles and amphibians at the Bronx Zoo. The reptile house is one of the most popular places in the zoo. It's Lisette's job to keep the animals looking—and feeling—their best. "There's something different every day, so the job is never boring," says Lisette. "Caring for the animals provides me with a lot of satisfaction."

Lisette holds a frilled lizard in the reptile house at the Bronx Zoo.

Name: Lisette Ramos

Hometown: Paterson, New Jersey

Job: Wild animal keeper, Bronx Zoo Herpetology (Reptile/Amphibian) Department

Duties:
• provides food and water
• builds zoo exhibits
• gives tours and lectures to visitors

Skills:
• ability to monitor and record health of animals
• public speaking skills
• physical fitness for lifting and restraining animals

Similar Jobs:
• vet technician
• zoo guide
• animal groomer

Pay: $29,000 and up per year

Education: College degree in biology

Ask Yourself

1. **Underline** ▶ Mark the skills you think you already have.

2. **Circle** ▶ Mark where Lisette works.

3. Would you want this job?
   ❏ I don't want it.
   ❏ I might want it.
   ❏ I really want it.

Reading a Public Notice

Lisette cares for reptiles at the Bronx Zoo. If a snake escaped from an exhibit, it would be Lisette's job to help track it down. Check out the warning sign about a brown tree snake on the loose. Then answer the questions below.

WARNING

Brown Tree Snake

Have you seen this snake? It is a brown tree snake that escaped from the Bronx Zoo. This reptile is an alien species to the New York area.

Distinguishing Characteristics:

❑ rear fangs

❑ a large head in relation to the body

❑ brownish or greenish coloring, with cross-band markings

❑ 18 inches to eight feet long

If Found:

• Protect any children in the area. A brown tree snake bite is mildly poisonous to adults but more harmful to children.

• Call the police. The brown tree snake is extremely dangerous to our environment.

▶ **Fill in the circle next to each correct answer.**

1. What is the purpose of this sign?
   Ⓐ to capture a criminal
   Ⓑ to alert the public
   Ⓒ to sell a pet
   Ⓓ to give care directions for a pet

2. How long are brown tree snakes?
   Ⓐ six feet long
   Ⓑ 18 inches long
   Ⓒ eight feet long
   Ⓓ anywhere from 18 inches to eight feet long

3. What should you do if you find one?
   Ⓐ Call the police.
   Ⓑ Kill it.
   Ⓒ Measure it.
   Ⓓ Take it to the police.

4. What would tell you that a snake is not a brown tree snake?
   Ⓐ It is brown.
   Ⓑ It is green.
   Ⓒ It is red.
   Ⓓ It has fangs.

5. What do you think "distinguishing characteristics" are?
   Ⓐ what the snake eats
   Ⓑ what the snake sounds like
   Ⓒ what the snake looks like
   Ⓓ how friendly the snake is

Comprehension

▶ **Fill in the circle next to the correct answer.**

1. What do snakehead fish eat?
- Ⓐ kudzu
- Ⓑ zebra mussels
- Ⓒ ants
- Ⓓ other fish

2. Which of these is an effect of the brown tree snakes?
- Ⓐ a great economy
- Ⓑ hundreds of power outages
- Ⓒ many birds and lizards
- Ⓓ all of the above

3. Which of these is an effect of invasive species?
- Ⓐ They kill native plants and animals.
- Ⓑ They ruin the food chain.
- Ⓒ They destroy the environment.
- Ⓓ All of the above.

> **Here's a tip.**
> Look for words like *cause*, *effect*, *problem*, and *solution* in questions. These cue words can help you figure out what kind of answer is expected.

4. Why has kudzu grown out of control?
- Ⓐ because people keep planting it everywhere
- Ⓑ because it thrives in the warm climate of the South
- Ⓒ because no one knows how to kill the plant
- Ⓓ because it kills fish in ponds all over the country

5. What can happen when an invader species interrupts a food chain?
- Ⓐ The invader eats food sources that other species need.
- Ⓑ The invaders are killed immediately.
- Ⓒ There's still plenty of food for every species to eat.
- Ⓓ The climate can change.

Vocabulary

▶ **Fill in the circle next to the correct definitions of the underlined words.**

1. Brown tree snakes have <u>altered</u> the <u>environment</u> of Guam.
   - Ⓐ left, city
   - Ⓑ infested, country
   - Ⓒ changed, habitat
   - Ⓓ taken over, homes

2. The snakehead fish <u>invaded</u> a pond in Maryland.
   - Ⓐ moved into and harmed
   - Ⓑ moved out
   - Ⓒ cleaned
   - Ⓓ ate

3. One <u>method</u> scientists use to kill invader <u>species</u> is poisoning them.
   - Ⓐ trick, aliens
   - Ⓑ payment of money, fish
   - Ⓒ way of doing something, kinds of animals
   - Ⓓ drug, plant

▶ **Fill in the circle next to the best answer.**

4. To be "in hot water" means to be in trouble. Which sentence uses this idiom correctly?
   - Ⓐ When Tamyra touched the boiling tea, she was in hot water.
   - Ⓑ Lianna was in hot water with her parents after coming home after curfew.
   - Ⓒ Michelle loves taking a bath in hot water.
   - Ⓓ To make soup, sprinkle powder into hot water.

▶ **How would the pronunciation guide in a dictionary show the underlined word?**

5. The fish <u>specimen</u> collected from that pond is very unusual.
   - Ⓐ spec-uh-man
   - Ⓑ speck-a-**meen**
   - Ⓒ **spess**-uh-muhn
   - Ⓓ **spess**-umme-n

Short Answer

▶ **Use what you've read in this Workshop to answer the question below. Check your spelling and grammar.**

What invasive species do you think is the worst for the U.S.? Why?

_____

_____

_____

_____

Turning Points

What does it mean to be "at a turning point"? It means getting ready for something totally new and different. Often, when teens make the transition into adulthood, they find themselves at a turning point.

Get ready to meet some amazing teens who have experienced a turning point—and triumphed. They have faced down tough challenges and turned their lives around.

VOCABULARY BUILDER

◎ Target Word ► Read the Target Words. Rate each one using the scale below.*	Meaning ► Read the Target Word meanings. Write in the missing ones.	Example ► Finish the Target Word examples below. Write in the missing ones.
attitude at•ti•tude (noun) ① ② ③		I have a good attitude about . . .
involve in•volve (verb) ① ② ③	to include someone or something	
label la•bel (noun) ① ② ③		Shy people can get the **label** of being stuck-up.
persist per•sist (verb) ① ② ③	to continue doing something even if it's difficult	
positive pos•i•tive (adjective) ① ② ③		This year, I'm positive that I will . . .

*Rating Scale
① = I don't know it at all.
② = I've seen it before.
③ = I know it and use it.

The Big Idea

Write ▶ What is this article mainly about?

_____

_____

_____

VOCABULARY BUILDER
Target Word

purpose

pur•pose (noun)

Rate it: ① ② ③

Meaning

_____

_____

Example

_____

_____

_____

React

Jonathan was given a label at school, and he didn't like it. Do students at your school label each other? Is that fair?

Starting Over

Moving to the U.S. changed everything

by Jonathan Fong

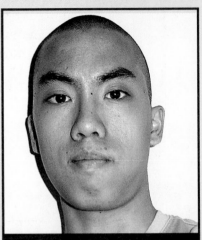

Jonathan Fong, high school student

I used to be one of the coolest guys in my school. But that was in Taiwan. In the U.S., classmates called me boring. Moving to the U.S. meant starting over.

I grew up in Taiwan, a small island near China. Then, four years ago, my mother sent me here for the **purpose** of getting a better education.

I worked hard at school in both Taiwan and the U.S. In Taiwan, my hard work paid off with good grades. However, in the U.S., school was a struggle. I didn't understand English. My grades suffered.

Finding new friends was even harder. I had always been outgoing and friendly. In Taiwan, I had a lot of friends. I went out all the time.

In the U.S., I was still outgoing, and I tried to make friends. But people didn't accept me. My new classmates thought I was totally uncool. Some people harassed me. They even gave me a label—the "boring foreign kid who didn't speak English."

I didn't let the label get me down. I knew that once I learned English, I'd be able to make friends. After a year in the U.S., my life is a lot better. I have friends. I am positive that I want to go to college in the U.S. Best of all, I no longer have a negative label. **END**

Words to Know!   **harassed** picked on or made fun of

Comprehension Focus

Compare and Contrast

When you **compare**, you tell how two things are the same. When you **contrast**, you tell how they are different. To compare and contrast:

- Ask yourself how two things are the same. Look for signal words such as *both*, *too*, *also*, and *in addition*.
- Ask yourself how two things are different. Look for signal words such as *but*, *rather than*, and *however*.

▶ **Fill in this chart to compare and contrast Jonathan's life in "Starting Over."**

Jonathan in Taiwan

Different
1. Jonathan was the cool, popular one.

2. _____

3. _____

Same
1. _____

2. _____

3. _____

Jonathan in the U.S.

Different
1. Kids thought that Jonathan was boring.

2. _____

3. _____

The Big Idea

Write What is this article mainly about?

_____
_____
_____
_____

VOCABULARY BUILDER
Target Word

initiate
i•ni•ti•ate (verb)

Rate it:

Meaning

_____
_____

Example

_____
_____
_____

 ## React

Ekiwah was dependent on others for many things. Why might being dependent be harder for a teen than for a little kid?

WORDS Set

This teen grew up unable to walk. He had a choice—to give up or to find a life that was uniquely his own.

Ekiwah Belendez Adler is the author of several books of poetry. Here, he sits at home with his father.

Him Free

Poetry can change lives. Sixteen-year-old Ekiwah (Eh-KEE-wah) Belendez Adler is living proof. Ekiwah was born with several serious diseases. He needed to use a wheelchair to get around. But when this teen discovered poetry, his life changed forever.

A Big Challenge

Ekiwah was born in a rural Mexican village. At birth, doctors said that he had cerebral palsy and paralytic scoliosis. These diseases bent his back and made his legs weak. They made him dependent on others—for everything.

When Ekiwah was little, kids his age played outside. Unlike his friends, Ekiwah had to stay inside. He couldn't walk without braces. He required help to perform simple tasks like walking down stairs. "I couldn't just go climb a tree," says Ekiwah.

As the years went by, Ekiwah felt like he was missing out on his youth. He didn't feel involved in the fun other kids were having. Finding happiness was a challenge.

Discovering Poetry

Ever since he was little, Ekiwah's parents read poetry to him. By the time he turned 10, Ekiwah was writing poetry himself. He was able to express his ideas and feelings. He discovered a talent that was all his own.

At age 12, Ekiwah published a book of poetry. At 14, he produced a second book. Two years later, his third book came out. Many people admired Ekiwah's unique voice. Suddenly, he felt connected to the world rather than isolated from it. He even **initiated** new friendships. ➡

Compare and Contrast

1. **Circle** ▶ Find the sentences that tell how Ekiwah and his friends were different.

2. **Write** ▶ Find two examples that show what happened to Ekiwah after he published three books of poetry.

- _____
_____
_____
_____
_____
_____

- _____
_____
_____
_____
_____

VOCABULARY BUILDER
Target Word

bond

bond (noun)

Rate it: ① ② ③

Meaning

_____

_____

Example

_____

_____

_____

 **React**

Write ▷ What do you think was the most important turning point in Ekiwah's life so far?

_____

_____

_____

_____

_____

_____

Still Suffering

By age 15, Ekiwah had become famous as a poet. But he was still suffering because of his curved spine. Doctors said that if it curved any more, it would affect Ekiwah's speech and breathing. They recommended immediate surgery.

Ekiwah's parents tried to find help. They sent Ekiwah's X-rays to Dr. Roy Nuzzo, a top surgeon in New York City. They also sent Ekiwah's poetry. Because Dr. Nuzzo was a poet, too, he felt a **bond** with Ekiwah. He offered to operate for free.

Road to Recovery

The operation took 10 hours. Doctors inserted rods, screws, and wires to alter Ekiwah's spine.

Now, Ekiwah's back feels better, and he can get around with a walker. Doctors are positive that Ekiwah is on the road to recovery.

Today, Ekiwah's life is very different than it was when he grew up. Rather than being dependent on others, Ekiwah can get around by himself. His home is still in Mexico. But now he travels around the world. While he remains close to his family, Ekiwah also has many friends and admirers.

Poetry has made a dramatic difference in Ekiwah's life. Words have truly set him free. ⟨END⟩

Words to Know! **dramatic** big and exciting

From the poem "Nothing" (abridged)
by Ekiwah Belendez Adler

I feel like a tree that has no branches
Like a warrior that has failed his mission.
Locked in a room with no door, no way out.
The earth like empty streets
No birds singing, only cars rushing by.

I feel like nothing.

The worst of criminals has come by
And robbed my smiles.

Compare and Contrast

▶ Fill in this chart to compare and contrast Ekiwah's life before and after poetry.

Ekiwah's Life Before

Different

1. _____

_____

_____

2. _____

_____

_____

3. _____

_____

_____

Same

1. _____

_____

_____

2. _____

_____

_____

3. _____

_____

_____

Ekiwah's Life After

Different

1. _____

_____

_____

2. _____

_____

_____

3. _____

_____

_____

The Big Idea

Write What is this article mainly about?

_____

_____

_____

_____

VOCABULARY BUILDER

Target Word

option

op•tion (noun)

Rate it: ① ② ③

Meaning

_____

_____

Example

_____

_____

_____

 React

Waila and Dali reacted differently to their mom's arrest. How would you react? More like Waila or more like Dali?

HARD

Two girls' lives were torn apart when their mom was put in prison. Only together could they build a new life.

An Empty Home

Four years ago, sisters Waila, 15, and Dali, 12, immigrated to New York from the Dominican Republic with their mom. They were poor. They didn't have many friends. And they didn't speak English. Their mom was under a lot of pressure to make ends meet. Her only **option** was to work 12 hours a day. Waila and Dali learned to take care of themselves.

One day, the sisters came home after school and waited for their mom. But she never came home. Later, they learned that she had been arrested and would have to serve a jail sentence.

Waila and Dali felt like their mom had abandoned them. They were confused and sad, but they were also angry.

Family friends helped take care of the girls. But sometimes, they had to fend for themselves. Their mom missed many holidays and birthdays. She also missed several important events, like Waila's high-school graduation and Dali's eighth-grade graduation.

Different Reactions

Even though Waila and Dali faced the same circumstances, they reacted differently to their mom's imprisonment. Waila didn't want anyone to know. She was embarrassed. She only

TIME

Dali and Waila learned to take care of themselves.

told her closest friends.

Dali, however, had a different attitude. She didn't care what other people thought. If people said bad things about her mom, Dali ignored them.

She didn't want anyone to pity them. "Nobody needs to feel sorry for us," she says. "We're doing fine."

The sisters were coping and surviving, each in her own way. ➡

Compare and Contrast

1. Write▶ How did the two sisters feel alike about their mom's imprisonment?

_____

_____

_____

_____

_____

2. Circle▶ Find the sentences that describe how the sisters reacted differently to their mom's imprisonment.

Review: Cause and Effect

Write▶ What caused Waila and Dali's mom to miss their graduations?

_____

_____

_____

_____

VOCABULARY BUILDER
Target Word

approximately

ap•prox•i•mate•ly *(adverb)*

Rate it:

Meaning

_____

_____

Example

_____

_____

_____

React

Write What would be the hardest thing about having a parent in jail?

_____

_____

_____

_____

_____

_____

A National Problem

There are kids like Waila and Dali all over the United States. Recent statistics show that more than 2 million kids have a parent in prison.

Most of these children have an incarcerated father. But the number of children with an incarcerated mother is soaring. From 1990 to 2000, the number of mothers in jail jumped 121 percent. Today, **approximately** 1 out of every 50 kids has a parent in prison. Like Waila and Dali, they have to struggle to put their lives back together.

A Fresh Start

Before their mother went to jail, Waila and Dali weren't that close to her. But after she went to jail, their mother really tried to be a better parent. She involved her daughters in a program called Hour Children. The program sets up visits between children and parents in jail. It provides activities and support to help the children with incarcerated parents.

The program helped both girls. Dali was able to express how hurt she was, having her mom in jail. She

 TEXT FEATURE **Reading a Line Graph**

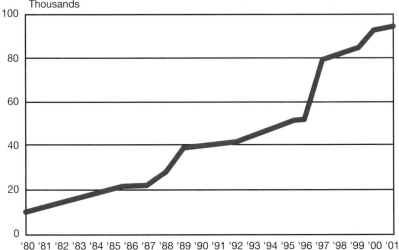

Source: Bureau of Justice Statistics, 2000

even started to write poetry. Waila's attitude was similar to her sister's. "I learned I could be myself," says Waila. "Being in the program made things a lot easier."

Finally, their mother was released from jail. But soon after, she was deported back to the Dominican Republic. Since then, the sisters have persisted in keeping their lives on the right track. Waila is preparing for college. Dali is in her high-school honor society.

The two sisters have made it past a tough turning point in their lives. They're excited about the future. And they're both positive about one thing—they don't have to make the mistakes their mom made. END

| Words to Know! | **deported** sent back to original country |

Waila and Dali visit their mom in jail.

A line graph shows how information changes over time.

1. When were there about 40,000 women in prison?
   Ⓐ 1982
   Ⓑ 1995
   Ⓒ 1989
   Ⓓ 1997

2. Which years had the sharpest increase of women in prison?
   Ⓐ 1980–1986
   Ⓑ 1986–1989
   Ⓒ 1996–1997
   Ⓓ 2000–2001

3. About how many more women were in prison in 1998 than in 1987?

_____

1. **Circle** ▶ What was Waila and Dali's relationship with their mom like before she went to prison?

2. **Write** ▶ How did their mom change after she went to prison?

_____
_____
_____
_____
_____
_____

✓ **Skills Check**

1. **Underline** ▶ How did Hour Children change Waila and Dali?

2. **Write** ▶ How are Waila and Dali different from their mom?

_____
_____
_____
_____
_____
_____

TAKE THE WORD CHALLENGE

Start

1

Think about it. What one mistake are you positive you'll never make?

_____

_____

_____

_____

_____

2

Choose. Which of the following labels fits your personality the best?

____ "a sports fanatic"

____ "a real techie"

____ "a movie nut"

____ "an out-of-control shopper"

3 Context Clues

Sometimes, you'll see a word you don't know in a sentence. One way to figure out what it means is to look at the words around it. These words are the "context" for the word. They can give you "context clues."

What do you think *excel* means? Study the context, and make a guess. Check the glossary to see if you got it right.

☐ to do poorly at something

☐ to give up on something

☐ to do something very well

☐ to quit doing something

I persisted at running. Now, I **excel** at it, man!

4

Evaluate. Your friend just lost another sports game. What would you say to help your friend keep a good attitude?

_____

_____

_____

5

Think about it. Approximately how long would you persist working on:

a hard video game   _____

a 500-piece puzzle   _____

trying to unlock a locker   _____

8 Noun Endings

To show more than one person, place, or thing, add an *-s* to most nouns.

- If a noun ends in *ss*, *s*, *x*, *ch*, or *sh*, add *-es* to make it plural, as in *buses* and *dresses*.

- If a noun ends in a consonant and *y*, change the *y* to *i* and add *-es* to make it plural, as in *spies*.

- Plus, watch out for irregular plurals like *mice*, the plural of *mouse*. These don't follow the rules!

Write the plural of each word below.

Singular	Plural
coach	_____
purpose	_____
dress	_____
penny	_____
foot	_____

6 Think about it. List three people (or pets!) you have a strong bond with.

1. _____

2. _____

3. _____

7 Your choice. If you had the option, which two events would you attend?

____ a World Series championship

____ the MTV Awards

____ a Hollywood movie premiere

____ the opening of a new Disney World

9 Fill in. If you could initiate a whole-school discussion on one important topic, what would that topic be?

_____

_____

10 Rate them. How much would you like to be involved in each of these activities?

	not at all	depends	very much
a deep-sea diving trip	____	____	____
a dance marathon	____	____	____
a wilderness race	____	____	____
a reality show on TV	____	____	____

Finish

Writing Focus

Descriptive Paragraph

A descriptive paragraph describes a person, place, thing, or event by using interesting and specific details.

▶ **Read Samir's descriptive paragraph about a person he admires.**

Student Model

My Basketball Coach

By Samir Campbell

The person I admire most is my coach, Liza Perez. Her appearance is surprising for a basketball coach. She's only five feet tall. In addition, her actions have given her a big reputation in this city. She has coached our team to three championships. Coach tells us that winning is more about teamwork than individual stars. Her motto is "The best players are team players." We listen, play together, and win. The thing I admire most about Coach is that she looks for the best in every player. She doesn't believe in labels--especially not "shorty." I'm glad I met Coach Perez. She taught me to think big, even if I'm not.

Parts of a Descriptive Paragraph

▶ Find these parts of Samir's descriptive paragraph.

1. Underline the sentence that tells **what is being described**.
2. Check three sentences with **descriptive details**.
3. Put a box around the descriptive details you think are most **interesting**.
4. Circle the **linking words** that connect the details.
5. Put a star beside the sentence that **sums** up the description and tells the writer's **feelings** about it.

Brainstorm

▶ **Read the writing prompt in the middle of the idea web. Then use the boxes to help you brainstorm your ideas.**

Appearance

Actions

Writing Prompt:
Describe a person whom you admire.

_____
(name)

Words

Personality Traits

Descriptive Paragraph | *Plan*

Plan Your Paragraph

Writing Prompt: Describe a person whom you admire.

▶ Use this chart to plan and organize your paragraph.

Word Choices

_____

_____

_____

_____

_____

Topic Sentence

• *The person I admire most . . .*

• *Ever since I met . . .*

• *I owe a lot to . . .*

Descriptive Detail

• *His/Her appearance . . .*

• *He/She is the most . . .*

• *He/She showed me how . . .*

Descriptive Detail

• *In addition, his/her actions . . .*

• *Also, his/her actions . . .*

• *The way he/she acts . . .*

Descriptive Detail

• *The thing I admire most . .*

• *Best of all . . .*

• *His/Her personality is . . .*

Conclusion

• *I'm glad I met . . .*

• *All in all, . . .*

• *I've never met another person who . . .*

Write Your Paragraph

▶ Use this writing frame to write a first draft of your paragraph.

The person I admire most _____ (title) _____

_____

_____

_____

His/Her appearance _____

_____

_____

In addition, his/her actions _____

_____

_____

_____

The thing I admire most _____

_____

_____

_____

I'm glad I met _____

_____

_____

_____

_____

Revise

▶ Rate your paragraph. Then have a writing partner rate it.

Scoring Guide			
weak	okay	good	strong
1	2	3	4

1. Does the beginning clearly state **what is being described**?

Self	1	2	3	4
Partner	1	2	3	4

2. Do the sentences contain **descriptive details**?

Self	1	2	3	4
Partner	1	2	3	4

3. Are the descriptive details **interesting**?

Self	1	2	3	4
Partner	1	2	3	4

4. Do **linking words** connect the details?

Self	1	2	3	4
Partner	1	2	3	4

5. Does the ending sentence **sum up** the description and tell the writer's **feelings** about it?

Self	1	2	3	4
Partner	1	2	3	4

▶ Now revise your paragraph to make it stronger.

Grammar USING ADJECTIVES THAT COMPARE

An **adjective** is a word that tells about or describes a noun. Adjectives can compare two or more people, places, or things.

- To use an adjective to compare two things, add *-er* to the adjective or use the word *more*.
- To use an adjective to compare three or more things, add *-est* to the adjective or use the word *most*.

Example

Adjective Comparing Two Things	Adjective Comparing Three or More Things
Ekiwah is happier than he was before.	He is the happiest boy in the world.
Ekiwah is more famous than his friend.	He is the most famous writer his age.

▶ **Circle the correct comparing word in the sentences below.**

1. Ekiwah was [(lonelier) loneliest] when he was young than he is now.

2. He was the [sicker sickest] child in his village.

3. Ekiwah faced [more most] hardship than I have.

4. Poetry became the [more most] inspiring thing in his life.

5. Ekiwah is also the [nicer nicest] person you could meet.

6. His life is [more most] rewarding than it was before he began writing.

▶ **Rewrite the sentences to compare three or more things correctly.**

7. Jonathan was the <u>more</u> outgoing boy in his school.

_____

8. His first year in America was the <u>tougher</u> of all.

_____

9. Jonathan is now the <u>happier</u> person in his class.

_____

10. Having a mom in prison was Waila's <u>bigger</u> problem.

_____

Take a close look at each of the sentences in your draft on page 199. Do they use adjectives that compare correctly? Fix the ones that don't.

Mechanics Using Quotation Marks

Quotation marks show the exact words of a speaker.

- The first word of a quotation is capitalized.
- Punctuation usually goes inside the ending quotation mark.

Example

Correct	Incorrect
Lisa yelled, "Way to go!"	Lisa yelled, "way to go!"
Josue said, "You did it!"	Josue said, "You did it"!

▶ **Find and correct five errors in this paragraph.**

Student Model

> One person who has changed my life is my cousin Rhondi. She is blind. She looks like other teenagers, but her life has been full of chalenges. Once, she told me that everyone thought she should be musical because she couldn't see. "No, she told them, I'm just a math whiz." The more interesting thing about Rhondi is her attitude. She's always possitive. I'm glad I know her!

Check and Correct

- ❏ Circle two spelling errors and correct them.
- ❏ Insert two missing quotation marks.
- ❏ Correct one error with a comparison.

Edit *Look at the sentences in your own draft on page 199. Do they all use quotation marks correctly? Fix the ones that don't.*

Final Draft/Present

▶ **Write a final draft of your paragraph on paper or the computer. Check it again and correct any errors before you present it.**

Personal Trainer

Kirk Miller is a personal trainer. He helps people get in shape or recover from accidents. He also helps his clients stay motivated in the gym— and in life. "When I train someone, I really care about them," he says. " I want them to be healthy and strong."

Name: Kirk Miller

Hometown: New York City

Job: Personal Trainer

Duties:
- develop fitness routines
- create healthy diets
- help clients organize their time and achieve their fitness goals

Skills:
- staying physically fit
- evaluating health and fitness of clients
- using workout equipment safely

Similar Jobs:
- physical therapist
- athletic coach
- dietician

Pay: $35,000 and up per year

Education: Bachelor's Degree, training in fitness and nutrition

Kirk Miller calls himself a "professional motivator." Here, he helps a client work out.

Ask Yourself

1. **Underline** ▶ Which duty would be easiest for you?

2. **Circle** ▶ In the "Skills" list, mark the skill you think you would need to work on the most.

3. How much do you want this job?

   ☐ I don't want it.

   ☐ I might want it.

   ☐ I really want it.

Analyzing a Nutrition Label

Kirk Miller's clients have lots of questions about the food they eat. He shows them how to read nutrition labels. He makes sure they get enough protein and not too much fat. Check out the label below.

▶ **Fill in the bubble next to the correct answer to each question.**

1. What makes up one serving of cookies?
   - Ⓐ one package
   - Ⓑ two packages
   - Ⓒ two cookies
   - Ⓓ four cookies

2. What percentage of your daily value of total fat does one serving have?
   - Ⓐ 3%
   - Ⓑ 13%
   - Ⓒ 11%
   - Ⓓ 7%

3. Which additional nutrients do you get when you eat these cookies?
   - Ⓐ vitamins A and C
   - Ⓑ a little iron
   - Ⓒ calcium and iron
   - Ⓓ vitamins A and C, plus calcium and iron

4. Fiber is important to your diet. How many grams (g) does one serving of cookies have?
   - Ⓐ Less than 1g
   - Ⓑ 20g
   - Ⓒ 10g
   - Ⓓ less than 5 mg

Nutrition Facts

Serving Size 4 cookies (29g)
Servings Per Container 2

Amount Per Serving

Calories 150   Calories from Fat 60

	% Daily Value*
Total Fat 7g	**11**%
Saturated Fat 2.5g	**13**%
Cholesterol less than 5mg	**1**%
Sodium 100mg	**4**%
Total Carbohydrate 20g	**7**%
Dietary Fiber less than 1g	**3**%
Sugars 10g	
Protein 2g	

Vitamin A 0%	•	Vitamin C 0%
Calcium 0%	•	Iron 4%

* Percent Daily Values are based on a 2,000 calorie diet. Your values may be higher or lower depending on your calorie needs.

5. Would it be healthy to eat these cookies at every meal? Why or why not?

_____

_____

_____

_____

Comprehension

► **Fill in the circle next to the correct answer.**

1. Jonathan Fong liked his life in Taiwan because _____.

Ⓐ he was popular and had lots of friends

Ⓑ no one liked him

Ⓒ he couldn't speak the language

Ⓓ the weather was nice

2. During his childhood, Ekiwah felt left out because _____.

Ⓐ he was smarter than everyone else

Ⓑ he didn't get along with his parents

Ⓒ he couldn't climb trees and play outside

Ⓓ all of the above

3. Which of the following is an example of how fame changed Ekiwah's life?

Ⓐ He was lonely.

Ⓑ He had many friends and admirers.

Ⓒ He couldn't walk.

Ⓓ He had to stay inside.

> **Here's a tip.**
> Read over your answers carefully. Double-check that you filled in the answers in the correct places.

4. How are Waila and Dali different?

Ⓐ They are both from the Dominican Republic.

Ⓑ They are sisters.

Ⓒ They had different reactions to their mom's imprisonment.

Ⓓ They both care about their mom.

5. When did Waila and Dali become close with their mom?

Ⓐ right before their mom went to prison

Ⓑ after their mom had gone to prison

Ⓒ after the girls had gone to prison

Ⓓ after the girls had graduated from high school

Vocabulary

▶ **Fill in the circle next to the correct definition of the underlined word.**

1. Did your teammates <u>involve</u> you in the pregame meeting?

Ⓐ include

Ⓒ applaud

Ⓑ remove

Ⓓ offend

2. Terry <u>persisted</u> at working on his comic book, even though he had an after-school job.

Ⓐ refused to do something

Ⓒ continued doing something

Ⓑ enjoyed doing something

Ⓓ appreciate something

3. I am <u>positive</u> that my sister is responsible for my <u>label</u> of "slob" at home.

Ⓐ unhappy, bedroom

Ⓒ delighted, collection

Ⓑ very sure, a word to describe someone

Ⓓ unsure, pet

▶ **Choose the word with the correct noun ending to complete this sentence.**

4. The boys' _____ about the sport changed once they started winning games.

Ⓐ attitudeses

Ⓒ attitudes

Ⓑ attitude

Ⓓ attiudies

▶ **Choose the correct definition of the underlined word using context clues.**

5. Terry had so many options for dessert, he found himself in a <u>dilemma</u>. He had to choose, but he didn't want to.

Ⓐ happy situation

Ⓒ options

Ⓑ food illness

Ⓓ difficult choice

Short Answer

▶ **Use what you've read in this Workshop to answer the question below. Check your spelling and grammar.**

Which person in this Workshop do you admire the most? Why?

_____

_____

_____

_____

_____

WORKSHOP 9

NONFICTION AND LITERATURE

Comprehension Focus
Make Inferences

READINGS
1 *Heartbeat of Harlem* >> Nonfiction Article
2 from *Bad Boy* >> Memoir
3 *Langston Hughes's Harlem* >> Poetry

THE STREETS OF HARLEM

It all began in the 1920s. Harlem was becoming the heartbeat of African-American culture. The streets were filled with excitement. Jazz musicians played the blues. Artists splashed colors onto canvas. Writers like Langston Hughes wrote poetry about being African American and living in Harlem. Other writers like Walter Dean Myers were growing up on its streets.

Take a walk back in time . . . on the streets of Harlem.

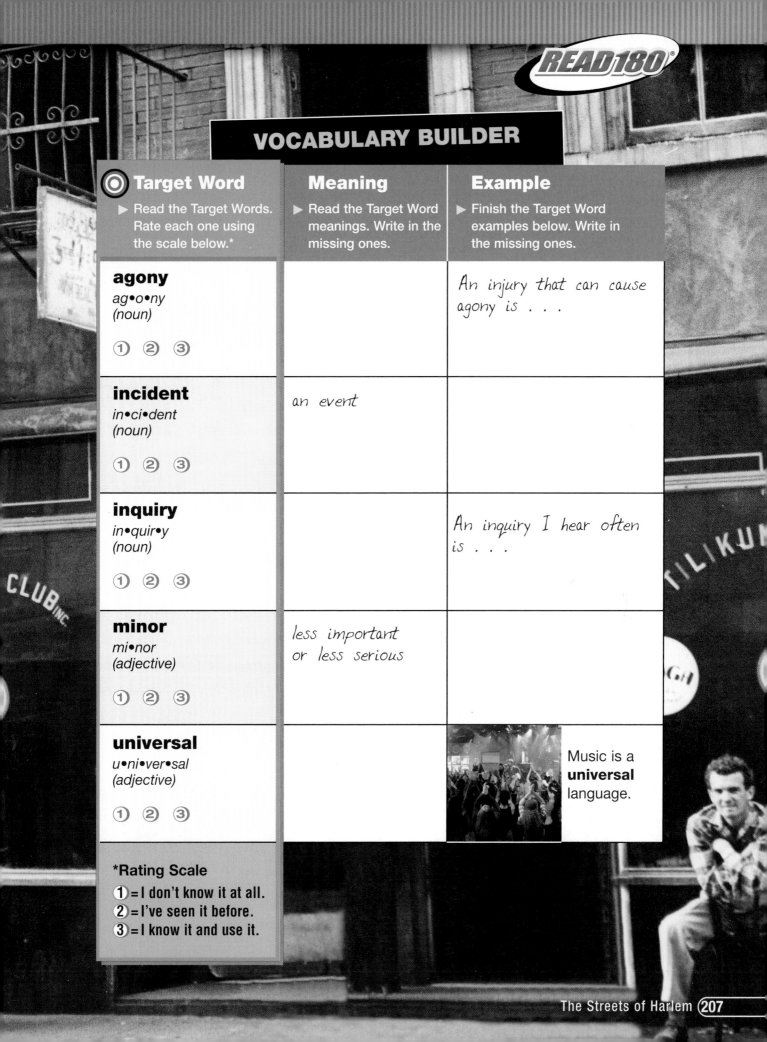

VOCABULARY BUILDER

◎ Target Word ▶ Read the Target Words. Rate each one using the scale below.*	Meaning ▶ Read the Target Word meanings. Write in the missing ones.	Example ▶ Finish the Target Word examples below. Write in the missing ones.
agony ag•o•ny *(noun)* ① ② ③		An injury that can cause agony is . . .
incident in•ci•dent *(noun)* ① ② ③	an event	
inquiry in•quir•y *(noun)* ① ② ③		An inquiry I hear often is . . .
minor mi•nor *(adjective)* ① ② ③	less important or less serious	
universal u•ni•ver•sal *(adjective)* ① ② ③		Music is a **universal** language.

*Rating Scale
① = I don't know it at all.
② = I've seen it before.
③ = I know it and use it.

The Big Idea

Write What is this article mainly about?

_____

_____

_____

VOCABULARY BUILDER
Target Word

resident

res•i•dent (noun)

Rate it: ① ② ③

Meaning

_____

_____

Example

_____

_____

_____

 React

What is the most interesting thing you learned about Harlem?

Heartbeat of Harlem

Harlem is a rectangle of city blocks at the top of Manhattan in New York City. From the 1920s to 1950s, this neighborhood's **residents** included many great African-American writers, musicians, and artists. They made Harlem famous through their writing, music, and art.

In the early 1900s, many African Americans moved from the South to the North. They were escaping racist laws and poverty. There were also more job options in the North. This movement was called the Great Migration.

Many people who came north settled in Harlem. By the 1920s and 1930s, Harlem had become the center of African-American culture. Painters and photographers captured images of the streets. Writers like Langston Hughes put new ideas to paper. And singers like

Music and dancing have always been a big part of Harlem life.

Ella Fitzgerald belted out the blues at the famous Apollo Theater.

Today, Harlem has something for everyone. Jazz and blues fill the air. Restaurants serve delicious Southern-style soul food. And neighborhood parks are filled with the dribbling beat of basketball games. In fact, the Harlem Globetrotters basketball team has been around for eighty years. They've slam dunked their way through more than 20,000 games!

Throughout its history, Harlem has had its ups and downs. But today, it's still one of the most exciting places in the world. **END**

Comprehension Focus
Make Inferences

When you **make inferences**, you form ideas about things that are not directly stated in the text. To make inferences:

- Look for a situation in the text in which the author gives clues but doesn't state exactly what is happening.
- Think about what you already know about the topic.
- Combine the text clues with your own experiences or knowledge to make an inference.

▶ **Fill in this chart to make an inference about "Heartbeat of Harlem."**

What I Learned From Reading

In the early 1900s, many African Americans moved from the South to escape racist laws and poverty.

_____

_____

_____

What I Already Know

_____

_____

_____

_____

_____

_____

_____

My Inference

_____

_____

_____

_____

_____

_____

_____

from

BAD

Write ▷ What is this memoir mainly about?

_____

_____

_____

❗ **React**

Write ▷ How would you describe your own neighborhood?

_____

_____

_____

_____

_____

_____

_____

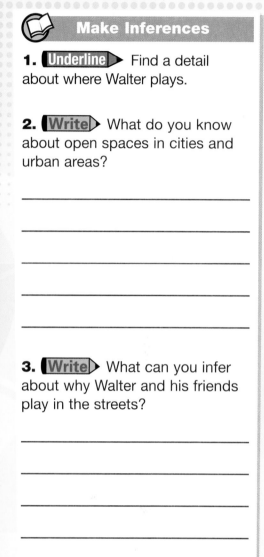

BOY
by Walter Dean Myers

Walter Dean Myers is a famous author. He grew up in Harlem in the 1940s and 1950s. In this excerpt from his memoir, Myers learns a very painful lesson.

PART I

I lived on Morningside Avenue, but I played mostly on the side streets because that's where the sewers were. The sewers were bases if you played stickball, they were the goal lines if you played football, they were base if you played tag, they were the spot you made your first shot from if you played skullies. The side street between Morningside Avenue and Manhattan Avenue was a pleasant block, lined with brownstones that had been converted into either single-room occupancies with community bathrooms or, at least, apartment dwellings that contained between four and six families. . . .

The whole block was guarded by Crazy Johnny, who had returned from the war kind of shell-shocked. If anything went wrong, Crazy Johnny would try to set it right. This usually meant trying to stop fights between kids and sweeping up broken bottles.

We didn't get many yellow cabs coming to the street, because downtown cabs didn't stop for black people and you didn't need to use a cab when the A train came directly to Harlem. One day in May there weren't any kids on the block to play with except Clyde Johnson, who was too young to play with. →

Words to Know! **converted** made into something else

Make Inferences

1. **Underline** ▷ Find a detail about where Walter plays.

2. **Write** ✎ What do you know about open spaces in cities and urban areas?

_____

_____

_____

_____

_____

3. **Write** ✎ What can you infer about why Walter and his friends play in the streets?

_____

_____

_____

_____

_____

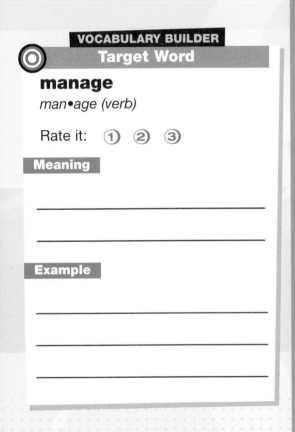

Active Reading

Write ▷ What does Walter do when he gets home?

_____

_____

_____

VOCABULARY BUILDER
Target Word

manage

man•age (verb)

Rate it: ① ② ③

Meaning

_____

_____

Example

_____

_____

_____

 React

What would you have done if you were Walter?

> "My jeans were in shreds at the knees, and the blood from my scraped knees was showing through. I tried to sit on the church steps, but the pain was too great."

A yellow cab pulled up in front of a building, and a fairly elegant looking lady got out. For some reason I thought it would be a good idea to hitch a ride on the back bumper of the cab. The cab started off with a jerk, and I was thrown off the bumper, but the sleeve of my shirt was caught. I was dragged the entire length of the block, bouncing along behind the cab, past the sewers, past parked cars, and all the way to the corner, where the cab was stopped by a light. It was there that I unhooked my sleeve and **managed** to get to my feet.

The agony was excruciating. Clyde asked me if I was hurt, and I said no.

"Your pants are torn," he said.

My jeans were in shreds at the knees, and the blood from my scraped knees was showing through. I tried to sit on the church steps, but the pain was too great. Stiff-leggedly I made my way around the corner and over to my building.

When I got home, Mama was on the phone and I went into the bathroom and got the iodine. Then I went to my room, stopping only to answer my mother's inquiry as to whether or not I was hungry.

"No, ma'am."

The iodine had a stopper and a glass rod applicator. I touched some iodine to my scraped leg. *Yow!* Enough of that. I went directly to bed.   ➡

Words to Know!   **excruciating** extremely painful

Comprehension Focus
Make Inferences

▶ **Fill in this chart to make inferences about Part I of "Bad Boy."**

What I Learned From Reading

Walter thought it would be a good idea to jump on the back of a cab.

What I Already Know

My Inference

What I Learned From Reading

Walter told both Clyde and his mother that nothing was wrong.

What I Already Know

My Inference

Active Reading

Star How does Walter say he got hurt?

VOCABULARY BUILDER

Target Word

reverse

re•verse (verb)

Rate it:

Meaning

_____

_____

Example

_____

_____

_____

 React

Write What do you think of the way Walter's mother handled the situation?

_____

_____

_____

_____

_____

_____

PART II

When Mama called me for supper that evening, I called back that I wasn't hungry. She called me a second time and told me to come to the kitchen, where my father now sat at the table, his dinner before him. By that time my legs had stiffened so I could hardly walk.

"What's wrong with you, boy?" my father asked.

"Nothing." My universal answer.

"What's wrong with you, boy?" My father's voice again, deeper, more resolute.

"My legs hurt," I said.

"Take your pants down."

Right there at the dinner table. I had changed pants and now undid my belt and gingerly let the changed pants down. My mother gasped when she saw my legs— a mass of bruises, swelling, and dried blood.

"What happened to you?" my father demanded.

I knew that hitching a ride on the back of a cab was wrong. And I had been trying so hard all year to be good. Maybe all these things were swimming around in my head too quickly. I honestly don't know what made me answer the way I did.

"Mama beat me with a stick," I said, the tears already flowing.

I think that if my mama hadn't been so shocked at the condition of my legs, she might have been able to respond. As it was, I don't think that she could really believe what she was hearing. First, there was her darling boy come home a bruised and bloody mess, in itself enough to send her into a blind panic, and then the same darling boy claiming to have suffered his injuries at her hand.

Words to Know! | **resolute** feeling strong and certain about something

Maybe I could have **reversed** myself, admitted what had really happened, if my father had not gone absolutely crazy with anger. He bellowed, "If you ever . . . how . . . why . . . If you ever touch him again I'll . . . " My father sputtered on and on. At this point Mama was crying. I was gingerly put into a hot bath to let my legs soak. I sat in the hot water and listened as my father hollered at Mama. It never occurred to him that I could be lying about such a thing. I went to bed and told God I was sorry.

The next two days I couldn't go to school. Mama brought me food and put it on a chair near my bed. She didn't say anything to me, just looked at me as if she had never seen me before. ➡

> "I knew that hitching a ride on the back of a cab was wrong. And I had been trying so hard all year to be good. Maybe all these things were swimming around in my head too quickly."

Make Inferences

1. [Underline] ▶ What does Walter say about how he got hurt?

2. [Write] ▶ How would you react if someone accused you of something you didn't do?

_____

_____

_____

_____

3. [Write] ▶ Walter's mother is silent. How might she be feeling on the inside?

_____

_____

_____

_____

Review:
Compare and Contrast

1. [Circle] ▶ How does Walter's father react to his explanation about the accident?

2. [Write] ▶ How does Walter's mother react differently to the explanation?

_____

_____

_____

_____

PART III

Two weeks later I was as good as new. Mama had been **instructed** by my dad not to touch me, and by the redness in his eyes she knew he meant it. I avoided *her* eyes when she asked how I could do such a thing to her. When she asked me what had really happened, I didn't answer. But Mama forgave me as usual, and I focused instead on the coming graduation from the sixth grade. My father checked my legs once a week because he hadn't forgotten the incident. Neither had God.

Eight days before graduation. We were playing stickball on 122nd Street, and a foul ball went up on the flat roof over the church vestibule. There was a drainpipe that came from the main roof and down the side of the church. Reverend Abbott, when he had been at the

church the summer before, had put barbed wire on the pipe to keep us from climbing it to get balls that went up there. We had ripped the wire down, and every kid on the block, girls included, could climb onto that roof. Up I went after the foul ball.

Enter Crazy Johnny.

"Get down from there!" he half yelled, half growled in his Crazy Johnny kind of way.

I threw the ball down, but I didn't come down. What I did instead was taunt Crazy Johnny from my perch. Johnny knew about the drainpipe and started climbing up after me. What Johnny didn't know was that I had a plan. ➡️

Words to Know!	**perch** a high place

Make Inferences

1. **Underline** ▷ Walter's mother asks how he could have done such a thing. Find a detail that shows Walter's reaction.

2. **Write** ▷ What do you know about how people act when they feel guilty?

_____

_____

_____

3. **Write** ▷ How is Walter feeling about what happened?

_____

_____

Active Reading

Star How does Walter get off the roof?

VOCABULARY BUILDER
Target Word

sustain

sus•tain (verb)

Rate it:

Meaning

_____

_____

Example

_____

_____

_____

React

Write Do you think Walter should have told his parents that he jumped off the roof? Why or why not?

_____

_____

_____

_____

_____

_____

Eric and I had watched enough war movies to know that if we ever got into the army, we were going to go airborne. Jumping out of a plane was fairly easy. You jumped, your parachute opened, and you floated down. In order not to hurt yourself on landing, you bent your knees, landed on your heels, and fell to one side.

 TEXT FEATURE Reading a Map

A neighborhood map shows the location of streets.

1. What information does this map show?
   Ⓐ New York City in 1999
   Ⓑ the state of New York
   Ⓒ Harlem during the Harlem Renaissance
   Ⓓ what Harlem will look like in the future

2. What river runs along the east side of Harlem?

   _____

3. What street is the Apollo Theater on?

   _____

Up came Crazy Johnny. My friends below screamed. I waited by the edge of the roof of the one-story building. I let Johnny get halfway across the roof before I jumped, my legs together and slightly bent. I landed on my heels, and the pain was unbearable.

Patty Lee and John Lightbourne, friends who lived on Morningside Avenue, helped me to the church steps, where I sat for a while before going home. I wanted desperately to tell somebody about the pain in my heels, but what could I say so soon after lying about the first incident? Oh, yes, I jumped off a roof? Mama beat me on the heels with a stick? I suffered in silence for the next two weeks. Years later I found out I had **sustained** minor fractures to both feet. END

Draw Conclusions

1. **Write** Based on Walter's two accidents, what conclusion can you draw about him?

_____

_____

_____

_____

_____

Skills Check

1. **Underline** Find two things Walter can't say about his latest injury.

2. **Write** How does it feel to lie or admit you did something wrong?

_____

_____

_____

_____

3. **Write** Why does Walter decide not to tell about his painful injury?

_____

_____

_____

_____

Active Reading

Write Who is the poet speaking to in the first poem?

_____

_____

_____

Langston Hughes's Harlem

Langston Hughes was a writer whose poetry was an important part of the Harlem Renaissance. What do his poems say about Harlem?

Juke Box Love Song

I could take the Harlem night

and wrap around you,

Take the neon lights and make a crown,

Take the Lenox Avenue busses,

Taxis, subways,

And for your love song tone their rumble down.

Take Harlem's heartbeat,

Make a drumbeat,

Put it on a record, let it whirl,

And while we listen to it play,

Dance with you till day—

Dance with you, my sweet brown Harlem girl.

React

Which poem do you like best? Why?

Harlem [2]

What happens to a dream deferred?

Does it dry up

like a raisin in the sun?

Or fester like a sore—

And then run?

Does it stink like rotten meat?

Or crust and sugar over—

like a syrupy sweet?

Maybe it just sags

like a heavy load.

Or does it explode?

Dreams

Hold fast to dreams

For if dreams die

Life is a broken-winged bird

That cannot fly.

Hold fast to dreams

For when dreams go

Life is a barren field

Frozen with snow.

Literary Elements: Similes

A **simile** is a comparison of two unlike things, using the words *like* or *as.* In "Harlem [2]," one simile is "like a raisin in the sun."

Circle ▶ Find two other similes in that poem.

Literary Elements: Metaphors

A **metaphor** is a comparison in which something is said to be something else. Metaphors use *is* or *was.* In "Dreams," one metaphor is "Life is a broken-winged bird."

Underline ▶ Find another metaphor in that poem.

TAKE THE WORD CHALLENGE

Start

1 Check. Which decisions would *your parents* want you to reverse?

- ☐ organizing your room
- ☐ not studying for a test
- ☐ eating a whole pizza
- ☐ getting a part-time job

. . . .

2 Tell. Have you ever been *really* surprised or scared? What was the incident? Go on—write about it.

_____

_____

_____

_____

_____

_____

I can't wait to tell my friends about this incident!

3 Multiple-Meaning Words

Multiple-meaning words are words that have more than one meaning. For example, *minor* means "less important or less serious." But it also means "someone under adult age."

Fill in these sentences with *jam, stuff,* or *present*.

> There's a **minor** problem. You're still a **minor**.

1. Don't wait for the future. Do it now, in the _____.

2. This garage is full of _____.

3. Here is your birthday _____.

4. Let's get some guitars and _____.

5. We will _____ my brother's piñata with his favorite candy.

6. Want some _____ on your toast?

4 Fill in. If I could manage to save enough money, I would

buy _____

_____

_____

. . . .

5 Fill in. Name three other residents on your block.

someone your age: _____

someone who lives next door: _____

someone who has a pet: _____

This is the worst headache I've ever had. I'm in agony!

6 Check. Which would cause you the most agony?

☐ a terrible headache

☐ a bad hair day

☐ a broken bone

☐ an empty wallet

· · · · · · · · · · · · · · · · · · ·

7 Rate it. Read the inquiries below. How often do you hear them?

1 = a lot
2 = sometimes
3 = never

____ "When will you be home?"

____ "What time is it?"

____ "Did you finish your homework?"

____ "Can I borrow a dollar?"

____ "Are you mad at me?"

8 Latin Roots

Our group has a **universal** goal. We want to **unite** all of the **universe**.

A **root** is a word or word part from another language that is the basis of an English word. The word *universal* comes from the Latin root *unus,* which means "one."

Fill in these sentences with *unicycle, uniform,* or *unique.*

1. I could tell she was a firefighter because she was wearing a

   _____.

2. A _____ is harder to ride than a bicycle.

3. That painting is _____.

9 Fill in. You need help. Who could instruct you in:

cooking a meal? _____

fixing a bicycle? _____

fixing a computer problem? _____

· · · · · · · · · · · · · · · · · · ·

10 Describe it. Write a caption for the photo below. Use the word sustain.

_____

_____

Finish

Writing Focus

Personal Narrative

A **personal narrative** tells about an event in the writer's life.

▶ **Read Teresa's personal narrative about an experience she had growing up in her neighborhood.**

Student Model

Riding Lessons
by Teresa Rodriguez

When I was five, my dad taught me how to ride a bike. He instructed me every night after dinner. First, we took my bike out into the alley behind our house. He held the bike while I tried to ride it. Next, he let go. Most of the time I lost my balance and fell, which was frustrating. I was lucky that I only got minor cuts and bruises. Finally, one time my dad let go, and I was off! I managed to ride around the block all by myself. Some of the neighbors were outside. When they saw me, they started clapping. I'll never forget that warm summer night when I took my first bike ride.

Parts of a Personal Narrative

▶ **Find these parts of Teresa's personal narrative.**

1. Underline the sentence that tells about the **event**.
2. Check three important **details** that tell about the event.
3. Number these details in the **time order** they happened.
4. Circle the **linking words** that connect the details.
5. Put a star before the sentence that **sums up** the event and tells the writer's **feelings** about it.

Brainstorm

▶ Read the writing prompt in the middle of the idea web. Then use the boxes to help you brainstorm your ideas.

With Your Family

With Your Neighbors

Writing Prompt:
Tell about an experience you had growing up in your neighborhood.

With Your Friends

At Your Favorite Neighborhood Places

The Streets of Harlem (225)

Plan Your Paragraph

Writing Prompt: Tell about an experience you had growing up in your neighborhood.

▶ Use this chart to plan and organize your paragraph.

Word Choices

_____

_____

_____

_____

_____

Event

• When I was . . .

• Once . . .

• One memory I have is . . .

Detail 1

• First, . . .

• To start with, . . .

• It all started when . . .

Detail 2

• Next, . . .

• Then, . . .

• After that, . . .

Detail 3

• Finally, . . .

• Then, . . .

• In the end, . . .

Ending

• I'll never forget . . .

• Looking back now, . . .

• This is a memory that . . .

Write Your Paragraph

▶ Use this writing frame to write a first draft of your paragraph.

_____
(title)

When I was_____

_____

_____

First,_____

_____

_____

Next,_____

_____

_____

Finally,_____

_____

_____

I'll never forget_____

_____

_____

_____

Revise

▶ Rate your paragraph. Then have a writing partner rate it.

Scoring Guide			
weak	okay	good	strong
1	2	3	4

1. Does the beginning clearly state the **event**?

Self	1	2	3	4
Partner	1	2	3	4

2. Are there **details** that tell about the event?

Self	1	2	3	4
Partner	1	2	3	4

3. Are the details arranged in the **time order** they happened?

Self	1	2	3	4
Partner	1	2	3	4

4. Do **linking words** connect the details?

Self	1	2	3	4
Partner	1	2	3	4

5. Does the ending **sum up** the event and tell the writer's **feelings** about it?

Self	1	2	3	4
Partner	1	2	3	4

▶ Now revise your paragraph to make it stronger.

Grammar USING ADVERBS

An **adjective** describes a person, place, or thing. An **adverb** describes a verb, an adjective, or another adverb. Many adverbs end in *-ly*.

- Use adverbs to make your writing more precise.

Example

Adjective	Adverb
I walked home at a **slow** pace.	I **slowly** walked home.
Crazy Johnny was not a **patient** person.	I waited **patiently** for Crazy Johnny.
A **quick** pain shot through my legs.	The pain shot **quickly** through my legs.

▶ **Circle the adverbs in the sentences below.**

1. My father shouted [angry (angrily)] when he saw my injury.

2. He went [**absolutely** **absolute**] crazy with anger.

3. My mother [**gentle** **gently**] treated my injuries.

4. My father checked my legs [**careful** **carefully**] after that.

5. The next day, I lay [**quietly** **quiet**] in bed.

6. I never told them what [**really** **real**] happened that day.

▶ **Rewrite the sentences using the correct form of the adverb.**

7. Jumping out of an airplane seemed <u>fair</u> easy.

_____

8. I leapt to the ground with my legs <u>slight</u> bent.

_____

9. I <u>desperate</u> wanted to tell someone about the pain.

_____

10. I suffered <u>silent</u> for the next two weeks.

_____

 Take a close look at each of the sentences in your draft on page 227. Do they use adverbs correctly? If not, fix them.

Usage CORRECTING SENTENCE FRAGMENTS

Each **sentence** must state a complete idea.

- You can often add a subject or a verb to a sentence fragment to form a complete sentence.

Example

Correct	Incorrect
Harlem is a great neighborhood to grow up in!	A great neighborhood to grow up in!

▶ Find and correct five errors in this paragraph.

Check and Correct

❑ Circle two spelling errors and correct them.

❑ Underline one incorrectly formed adverb and correct it.

❑ Correct two sentence fragments.

Student Model

When I was nine, a fire broke out. In my neighborhood. It started when my neighbor forgot to turn off his iron. ran out of his house yelling "Fire!" After that, someone quick called the fire department. All the residants of the block stared at the flames. In the end, the fire was put out, and there were no injuries. The memory of this insident will always stay with me.

 Edit *Look at the sentences in your own draft on page 227. Do they all contain a subject and a verb? If not, fix them.*

Final Draft/Present

▶ **Write a final draft of your paragraph on paper or the computer. Check it again and correct any errors before you present it.**

WALTER DEAN MYERS

Walter Dean Myers had a hard life. After his mother died, he was raised in Harlem by foster parents. In school, he struggled because of a speech problem. He misbehaved and got into a lot of trouble. Eventually, Myers joined the army.

After he left the army, Myers worked low-paying, difficult jobs. But one day his life changed. He entered a children's book-writing contest. He won the contest with the book *Where Does the Day Go?* Since then, Myers has never looked back. He has become one of America's favorite authors for young adults.

Books: *Bad Boy, Harlem, Somewhere in the Darkness, The Greatest: Muhammad Ali*

"The public library was my most treasured place. I couldn't believe my luck in discovering that what I enjoyed most—reading—was free."

Langston Hughes

Langston Hughes was a lifelong writer. Born in 1902, he wrote his first poem in the eighth grade. But Hughes's father said writing wouldn't pay the bills. So Hughes went to Columbia University to study engineering. But eventually, he dropped out. He realized that writing was his calling.

Hughes's first book was published in 1926. In the same year, he entered Lincoln University. He graduated in 1929 with a bachelor's degree. Later, Hughes moved to Harlem, where he listened to jazz music and wrote poetry until his death in 1967.

Books: *The Best of Simple, The Big Sea, The Dream Keeper and Other Poems, Not Without Laughter*

"No great poet has ever been afraid of being himself."

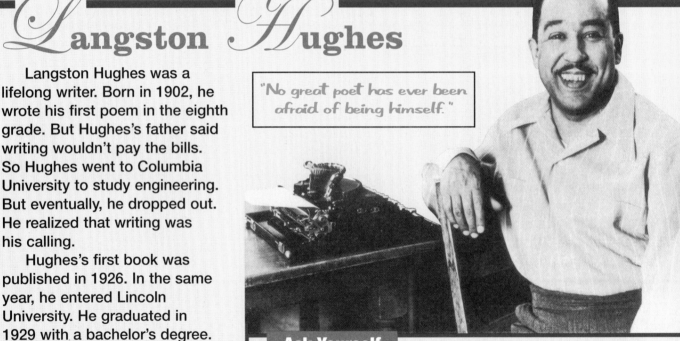

Ask Yourself

1. **Underline** ▶ Why did Myers struggle in school?

2. **Circle** ▶ When was Hughes's first book published?

3. Which author would you like to learn more about? Explain.

_____

_____

Reading a Web Site

Where can you learn more about the Harlem Renaissance? The Internet is a good place to start. Check out the Web site below.

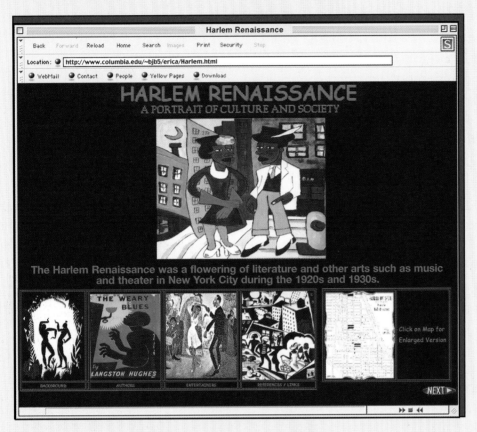

▶ **Fill in the circle next to each correct answer.**

1. What is the name of this Web site?

Ⓐ Background

Ⓑ Harlem Renaissance

Ⓒ Next

Ⓓ References/Links

2. What information about the Harlem Renaissance is on this site?

Ⓐ culture and society

Ⓑ politicians

Ⓒ weather patterns

Ⓓ history of Harlem in the 1820s

3. What will happen if you click on the map?

Ⓐ It will get smaller.

Ⓑ It will disappear.

Ⓒ It will get bigger.

Ⓓ Nothing will happen.

4. Which button would you click to find information about writers from the Harlem Renaissance?

Ⓐ Authors

Ⓑ Entertainers

Ⓒ Next

Ⓓ Background

5. What are you most likely to see if you click "References/Links"?

Ⓐ photos of Harlem

Ⓑ book titles and links to other Web sites

Ⓒ a poem by Langston Hughes

Ⓓ the Web site's home page

Comprehension

▶ **Fill in the circle next to the correct answer.**

1. In "Bad Boy," what was Walter's main problem?

   Ⓐ He was the new kid in school.

   Ⓑ He got hurt and lied about it.

   Ⓒ His neighborhood was getting crowded.

   Ⓓ His family was moving away.

2. Langston Hughes probably wrote poems about dreams to

   Ⓐ help people who have trouble sleeping.

   Ⓑ give people positive feelings about nature.

   Ⓒ write about a boring topic.

   Ⓓ inspire people to follow their dreams.

> **Here's a tip.**
> Check your work against the reading you're being tested on. Make sure your answer agrees with what's in the reading.

3. How are all the readings in this Workshop similar?

   Ⓐ They are all about Harlem.

   Ⓑ They all involve young teens.

   Ⓒ They are all poems.

   Ⓓ They are all about the future.

4. Based on this Workshop, which of the following statements about the Harlem Renaissance is true?

   Ⓐ Nobody wanted to live in Harlem.

   Ⓑ People were not encouraged to use their talents.

   Ⓒ There was a lot of discrimination in Harlem.

   Ⓓ It was an exciting, creative time in Harlem's history.

5. Which of the following could be included in this Workshop?

   Ⓐ a nonfiction article about dancing

   Ⓑ a short story about a girl in Harlem

   Ⓒ a poem about nightmares

   Ⓓ a photo essay about cities

Vocabulary

▶ **Fill in the circle next to the correct definition of the underlined word.**

1. Being dragged by a cab is an <u>incident</u> that Walter Dean Myers never forgot.

   Ⓐ story   Ⓒ dream
   Ⓑ joke   Ⓓ event

2. Walter Dean Myers was in <u>agony</u> from his cuts and bruises.

   Ⓐ pain   Ⓒ trouble
   Ⓑ loneliness Ⓓ laughter

3. He didn't want to answer his father's <u>inquiry</u> about how he got hurt.

   Ⓐ complaint   Ⓒ lie
   Ⓑ question   Ⓓ answer

▶ **Choose the correct definition for the underlined multiple-meaning word.**

4. Walter's injuries were <u>minor</u>. They could have been a lot worse.

   Ⓐ under the age of eighteen   Ⓒ less serious
   Ⓑ a subject that you study   Ⓓ major

▶ **Choose the correct word to fill in the blank.**

5. Walter's _____ answer to everything was "Nothing."

   Ⓐ unicycle   Ⓒ universal
   Ⓑ universe   Ⓓ university

Short Answer

▶ **Use what you've read in this Workshop to answer the question below. Check your spelling and grammar.**

Describe Harlem, giving at least two details from the readings.

_____

_____

_____

_____

_____

Glossary

A glossary is a useful tool found at the back of many books. It contains information about key words in the text. Look at the sample glossary entry below.

This is an **entry word**—the word you look up. It is divided into syllables.

The **pronunciation** comes after the entry word. Letters and letter combinations stand for different sounds. The accented syllable is marked in boldfaced letters.

This tells you what **part of speech** the entry word is.

cy•cle (**sye**-kuhl)

1. *noun* A sequence of events that repeats itself. *The seasons follow the same cycle every year.*
2. *verb* To ride a bicycle. *I like to cycle in the park with my friends.*

A **number** appears at the beginning of each meaning when more than one meaning is given for the entry word.

Look here to find the **meaning** of the entry word.

cycle

a·ban·don
(uh-**ban**-duhn) *verb*
To leave behind. *The sailors had to abandon the ship when it sank.*

ag·o·ny
(**ag**-uh-nee) *noun*
Great pain or suffering. *After he fell, Rashawn screamed in agony.*

al·ter
(**awl**-tur) *verb*
To change in some way. *The builder altered the house by adding a front porch.*

anx·i·e·ty
(ang-**zye**-uh-tee) *noun*
A strong feeling of worry. *The thought of another test filled Theresa with anxiety.*

ap·pre·ci·ate
(uh-**pree**-shee-*ate*) *verb*
To like and feel grateful for something. *I always appreciate it when someone gives me a present.*

ap·prox·i·mate·ly
(uh-**prok**-si-muht-lee) *adverb*
An estimate; more or less than an exact number. *We need approximately two days to finish the project.*

as·sist
(uh-**sisst**)
1. *verb* To help. *I like to assist my mom with dinner.*
2. *noun* A play or pass that helps a teammate score. *Freddy made two assists in the championship game.*

as·sure
(uh-**shur**) *verb*
To promise. *I assure you that I will be at the party on time.*

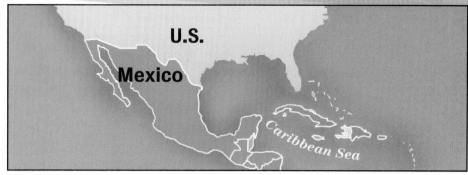

border

at·ti·tude
(**at**-i-tood) *noun*
1. An opinion or feeling about something. *Alicia has a positive attitude about her work.*
2. (*slang*) A bossy or stuck-up manner. *Once she was famous, she developed an attitude.*

au·thor·i·ty
(uh-**thor**-uh-tee) *noun*
Someone who knows a lot about something. *The zoologist is an authority on polar bears.*

ben·e·fit
(**ben**-uh-fit) *noun*
1. A good result. *Good health is a benefit of eating well.*
2. A performance to raise money for a charity. *We held a benefit for our school band.*

bi·zarre
(bi-**zar**) *adjective*
Very strange. *His haircut was bizarre, with five colors and six different lengths of hair.*

bond
(**bond**)
1. *noun* A feeling that unites people or groups. *My brother and I are twins, so we have a strong bond.*
2. *verb* To stick together. *Glue bonds paper together.*

bor·der
(**bor**-dur) *noun*
The line that divides two countries. *The border between the U.S. and Mexico is in the southwest part of the U.S.*

brawl
(**brawl**) *verb*
To fight in a noisy way. *The two dogs brawl whenever they see each other.*

ca·pa·ble
(**kay**-puh-buhl) *adjective*
Able to do something. *My younger sister is capable of taking care of herself.*

Prefixes
Incapable begins with the prefix *in-*, meaning "not." A **prefix** is a letter or group of letters added to the beginning of a word. A prefix changes the meaning of a word. *Incapable* means "not able to do something."

climate

cli·mate
(**klye**-mit) *noun*
Weather conditions. *The climate where seals live is usually very cold.*

com·mu·ni·cate
(kuh-**myoo**-nuh-kate) *verb*
To share information. *Sam prefers to communicate by phone.*

con·spic·u·ous
(khun-**spik**-yoo-uhss) *adjective*
Very easy to notice. *Her absence from the party was conspicuous.*

con·stant
(**kon**-stuhnt) *adjective*
All the time. *My clock makes a constant ticking noise.*

con·vert
(kuhn-**vurt**) *verb*
To make into something else. *We want to convert our basement into a guest room.*

con·vince
(kuhn-**vinss**) *verb*
To make someone believe or do something. *I had to convince my parents to let me stay out late.*

cur·rent·ly
(**kur**-uhnt-lee) *adverb*
At the present time. *My mom currently works at the mall.*

cy·cle
(**sye**-kuhl)
1. *noun* A sequence of events that repeats itself. *The seasons follow the same cycle every year.*
2. *verb* To ride a bicycle. *I like to cycle in the park with my friends.*

Compound Words

Motorcycle **is a compound word. A compound word is made up of two smaller words, like** *motor+cycle***.**

de·ceive
(di-**seev**) *verb*
To trick. *I can deceive my brother into giving his candy to me.*

de·fer
(di-**fur**) *verb*
To delay. *We had to defer our trip by a week due to bad weather.*

de·gree
(di-**gree**) *noun*
1. A unit of measurement. *The temperature went up five degrees this afternoon.*
2. A title given by a college or university, such as a degree in medicine. *Diane received her law degree from the University of Texas.*

de·pend
(di-**pend**) *verb*
To count on. *I depend on my dad to take me to soccer practice.*

de·port
(di-**port**) *verb*
To send someone back to their original country. *The government is going to deport my uncle if he doesn't find a job.*

de·press·ing
(di-**press**-ing) *adjective*
Making you feel sad. *A dark, rainy day can be depressing.*

de·prive
(di-**prive**) *verb*
To not give someone something they need. *No one should deprive a dog of food or water.*

de·spair
(di-**spair**) *noun*
A feeling of being very unhappy and having no hope. *After Lisa's parents died, she was full of despair.*

de·struc·tion
(di-**struhk**-shuhn) *noun*
Terrible damage. *The tornado caused destruction all over town.*

destruction

dra·mat·ic
(druh-**mat**-ik) *adjective*
Very large or exciting. *Dianne wanted a dramatic change in her looks, so she dyed her hair.*

e·con·o·my
(i-**kon**-uh-mee) *noun*
The way money is made and shared. *When the economy is bad, people often lose their jobs.*

en·vi·ron·ment
(en-**vye**-ruhn-muhnt) *noun*
Surroundings or habitat. *I like to do my homework in a quiet environment.*

er·ror
(**er**-ur) *noun*
A mistake. *Tina made only one error on the test.*

e·vac·u·ate
(i-**vak**-yoo-ate) *verb*
To leave due to an emergency. *We had to evacuate because of the flood.*

evacuate

ev·i·dent
(**ev**-uh-duhnt) *adjective*
Easily noticed or understood. *It is evident that you don't believe what I'm saying.*

ex·ceed
(ek-**seed**) *verb*
To be greater than something. *If you exceed the speed limit, you'll get a ticket.*

ex·cru·ci·a·ting
(ek-**skroo**-shee-*ay*-ting) *adjective*
Extremely painful. *The pain from this cavity is excruciating.*

ex·haust
(eg-**zawst**) *verb*
To tire out. *A marathon can exhaust even a great runner.*

exhaust

ex·pand
(ek-**spand**) *verb*
1. To get bigger. *The balloon will expand when you fill it with air.*
2. To add more details to something you've already said. *I will expand on my idea in a speech.*

fo·cus
(**foh**-kuhss) *verb*
1. To pay close attention. *I need you to focus on these directions.*
2. To change the position of a camera lens so you can see something clearly. *I focused my lens on the flower and took a picture.*

gen·u·ine·ly
(**jen**-yoo-uhn-lee) *adverb*
Truly or sincerely. *I genuinely believe that she's telling the truth.*

gust
(**guhst**) *noun*
A sudden, strong movement of wind. *A gust of wind knocked that tree down.*

har·ass
(huh-**rass**) *verb*
To pick on or make fun of. *My older brother likes to harass me.*

i·den·ti·ty
(eye-**den**-ti-tee) *noun*
Who a person is. *I had to show proof of my identity to get on the plane.*

im·age
(**im**-ij) *noun*
1. How a person appears to other people. *Based on his image, you would think he is nice.*
2. A picture formed in a lens, TV, or mirror. *The image of children singing lit up the TV.*

Idioms
Someone who looks just like his dad can be "the spitting image" of his father. "Spitting image" is an **idiom**, an expression that means something different from the separate words.

im·mi·grant
(**im**-uh-gruhnt) *noun*
Someone who moves from one country to another. *My grandfather was an immigrant from Mexico.*

im·pact
(**im**-pakt) *noun*
The effect an event has on someone or something. *Opening the store early had a huge impact on sales that day.*

im·pos·tor
(im-**poss**-tur) *noun*
Someone who pretends to be someone else. *An Elvis look-alike is an impostor.*

impostor

im·press
(im-**press**) *verb*
To make someone admire something. *I want to impress all my friends with my new outfit.*

in·ci·dent
(**in**-suh-duhnt) *noun*
An event. *The mall was shut down for a day because of an incident involving teen violence.*

in·come
(**in**-kuhm) *noun*
Money from a job. *I worked more this year, so my income was higher.*

in·crease
(in-**kreess**) *verb*
To make or get larger. *To increase her muscles, Ashley works out every day.*

in·flu·ence
(**in**-floo-uhnss) *verb*
To change or affect something. *My aunt, a hairdresser, influences me to take better care of my hair.*

i·ni·ti·ate
(i-**nish**-ee-ate) *verb*
To start something. *My goal this school year is to initiate a new friendship with someone.*

Synonyms

To **initiate** is "to start something" and to **commence** is "to begin or start something." These words are **synonyms**, words that have similar meanings.

in·quir·y
(in-**kwye**-ree) *noun*
A question. *I addressed my inquiry about the ripped jeans to the store owner.*

instruct

in·struct
(in-**struhkt**) *verb*
To teach. *The coach will instruct the team on how to pass the ball.*

in·tense
(in-**tenss**) *adjective*
Having a strong effect. *The intense fire was strong enough to heat the whole house.*

in·ter·fere
(*in*-tur-**fihr**) *verb*
To deliberately get involved in a situation where you are not wanted or needed. *My friends often interfere when they think I'm making a mistake.*

in·ter·na·tion·al
(*in*-tur-**nash**-uh-nuhl) *adjective*
Being from two or more countries. *The United Nations is an international organization.*

international

in·vade

(in-**vade**) *verb*

To move into and harm. *The soldiers tried to invade the fort.*

Suffixes

Invasion ends with the suffix *-ion*. A **suffix** is a letter or group of letters added to the end of a word. The suffix *-ion* changes *invade* from a verb to a noun.

in·volve

(in-**volv**) *verb*

To include or be a part of something. *I want to involve all my friends in planning my party.*

i·so·lat·ed

(**eye**-suh-late-id) *adjective*

1. All alone. *I felt isolated when my two best friends moved away.*
2. Far away from other things. *The star was isolated in millions of miles of empty space.*

la·bel

(**lay**-buhl) *noun*

A word or phrase used to describe someone or something. *My T-shirt has a label on it.*

label

labor

la·bor

(**lay**-bur) *noun*

Hard work. *Child labor is an issue in many countries.*

lin·ger

(**ling**-gur) *verb*

To wait around. *Ashley will linger by the concert stage door until her favorite singer finally comes out.*

lux·u·ry

(**luhk**-shuh-ree) *noun*

Something very rich and special. *Christopher loved the look of luxury, so he bought himself fancy designer clothes.*

ma·jor

(**may**-jur)

1. *adjective* Very large or important. *I studied all weekend for a major science test.*
2. *noun* The main subject you study at college. *My major in college was communications.*

man·age

(**man**-ij) *verb*

To be able to do something that is hard. *With training, I can manage to run a marathon.*

man·u·al

(**man**-yoo-uhl)

1. *adjective* By hand. *It was hard work getting water from the manual pump.*
2. *noun* A set of instructions that tell how to use something. *We used the manual to fix our stereo.*

Root Words

The word *manual* comes from the Latin root *manus* which means "hand." A **root** is a word or word part from another language that is the basis of an English word.

men·tal

(**men**-tuhl) *adjective*

Having to do with the mind. *Getting ready for a test takes a lot of mental energy.*

men·tor

(**men**-tor) *noun*

Someone who offers help and guidance. *My mentor helped me learn how to succeed at my first job.*

me·tal·lic

(muh-**tal**-ik) *adjective*

Made of metal. *My sister likes to wear metallic jewelry.*

meth·od
(**meth**-uhd) *noun*
A way of doing something. *One method of getting a stain out is to pour vinegar on it.*

min·i·mum
(**min**-uh-muhm) *adjective*
The least amount. *My mom got mad when I did the minimum amount to help her.*

mi·nor
(**mye**-nur)
1. *adjective* Less important or less serious. *Joe had a minor cut so he didn't go to the doctor.*
2. *noun* Someone under the age of eighteen. *Minors are not allowed to vote in elections.*

Homophones

***Minor* means "less important" and *miner* means "a person who digs for coal or other minerals." These are homophones, words that sound alike but have different spellings and meanings.**

mi·nor·i·ty
(muh-**nor**-uh-tee) *noun*
A group that is less than half of the whole. *Most students like pizza, but a minority of them don't.*

moist
(**moist**) *adjective*
Damp. *Please wipe the table down with a moist cloth.*

monitor

mon·i·tor
(**mon**-uh-tur)
1. *verb* To track or follow. *My coach wants to monitor my progress for the next two years.*
2. *noun* A piece of equipment that shows information on a screen. *Artists work on large computer monitors.*

mo·ti·vate
(**moh**-tuh-vate) *verb*
To make someone want to do something. *Our coach motivates us to win by giving us pep talks.*

mul·ti·ply
(**muhl**-tuh-*plye*) *verb*
To grow in number rapidly. *I want to kill all the weeds before they multiply.*

na·tive
(**nay**-tiv) *noun*
Originally from an area. *My best friend is a native of Ohio.*

neg·a·tive
(**neg**-uh-tiv) *adjective*
1. Bad. *After she stole the ring, we all had a negative opinion of her.*
2. Giving the answer "no." *I asked Jaden if he wanted to go to the movies, but his reply was negative.*

op·tion
(**op**-shuhn) *noun*
A choice. *The teacher gave us more than one option for our project.*

Noun Endings

To make a noun plural, most nouns just need an *s*, like *options*. But nouns that already end in an *s* need –*es*, like *buses*. Nouns that end in *y* need –*ies*, like *policies*.

par·ti·ci·pate
(par-**tiss**-uh-*pate*) *verb*
To be a part of something. *I want to participate in as many after-school activities as possible.*

pe·cu·liar
(pi-**kyoo**-lyur) *adjective*
Strange. *Sometimes I hear peculiar noises at our cabin.*

per·cent
(pur-**sent**) *noun*
A part of a whole. *Eighty percent of the students went to the dance.*

perch
(**purch**) *noun*
A high place. *The bird's favorite perch was my windowsill.*

per·sist

(pur-**sist**) *verb*

To continue to do something, even though it is difficult. *I will persist in searching for a job until I find one.*

phe·nom·e·non

(fe-**nom**-uh-non) *noun*

An event of scientific interest. *The astronomer studied the phenomenon of the comet that appeared every eighty years.*

phenomenon

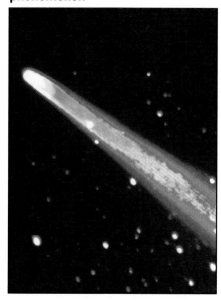

pit·y

(**pit**-ee) *verb*

To feel sorry for someone. *I pity people who are homeless during bad weather.*

poi·son·ous

(**poi**-zuhn-uhss) *adjective*

Containing poison that is dangerous. *Don't eat wild berries because they may be poisonous.*

pol·i·cy

(**pol**-uh-see) *noun*

A rule. *Our school has a policy against bringing pets to class.*

pos·i·tive

(**poz**-uh-tiv) *adjective*

Very sure that something is right or good. *Joe was positive his team was going to win the game.*

pre·cise·ly

(pri-**sisse**-lee) *adverb*

Exactly. *We left for the airport at precisely 4:15 PM.*

pres·sure

(**presh**-ur) *noun*

A force or stressful demand. *The clerk was under a lot of pressure to make many sales.*

pre·vent

(pri-**vent**) *verb*

To stop from happening. *Brushing your teeth will help prevent tooth decay.*

prin·ci·ple

(**prin**-suh-puhl) *noun*

A basic truth or belief. *Our country was founded on the principle of equality.*

pro·duce

1. (pruh-**dooss**) *verb* To make something. *They produce cars at that factory.*
2. (**prod**-ooss) *noun* Food that has been grown or farmed, such as fruits and vegetables. *Produce tastes best when it's fresh, not frozen.*

pur·pose

(**pur**-puhss) *noun*

Reason for doing something. *My purpose for mowing lawns is to earn some money.*

quiv·er

(**kwiv**-ur) *verb*

To shake. *A cold chill ran down my spine, and I began to quiver.*

Multiple-Meaning Words

Quiver means "to shake." It also means "a portable case for holding arrows." Multiple-meaning words are words that have more than one meaning.

re·bel

1. (ri-**bel**) *verb* To act out against. *Some teenagers feel the need to rebel against their parents.*
2. (**reb**-ul) *noun* Someone who fights against a government or the people in charge of something. *The rebels closed in on the army headquarters.*

rebel

rec·og·nize

(**rek**-uhg-*nize*) *verb*

To see someone and know who the person is. *My friend loves to recognize celebrities on the street.*

rec·om·mend

(rek-uh-**mend**) *verb*

To advise someone to do something. *The book is so good, I recommend that everyone reads it.*

re·cov·er·y

(ri-**kuhv**-ur-ee) *noun*

The process of getting back to normal. *The doctor said Tom's recovery from the accident would be quick.*

re·form

(ri-**form**) *verb*

To make something better by changing it. *Some people want to reform tax laws.*

re·in·force

(ree-in-**forss**) *verb*

To make something stronger. *We have to reinforce our skating ramp before it's safe to skate on.*

re·ject

1. (ri-**jekt**) *verb* To turn down. *I will reject the job offer because the job seems boring.*
2. (**ree**-jekt) *noun* Something that has been thrown away. *I chose two peaches that were still fresh and put six rejects in the garbage.*

re·lease

(ri-**leess**) *verb*

To let someone or something be free. *I always release a fish right after I catch it.*

re·move

(ri-**moov**) *verb*

To take something away. *Please remove the plates when we are finished eating.*

re·quire

(ri-**kwire**) *verb*

To make someone do something. *Most restaurants require customers to wear shoes.*

re·side

(ri-**zide**) *verb*

To live in a particular place. *Not many young people reside in my building.*

res·i·dent

(**rez**-uh-duhnt) *noun*

Someone who lives in a particular place. *The residents like to sit in front of their house.*

residents

res·o·lute

(**rez**-uh-loot) *adjective*

Feeling strong and certain about something. *José argued with his parents about going to the party, but they were resolute in their decision that he had to stay home.*

re·sourc·es

(ri-**sorss**-ez) *noun*

Things that you need to do something. *The library has lots of great resources for research papers.*

re·spond

(ri-**spond**) *verb*

To react to something that has been said or done. *I need to respond to my cousin's letter.*

re·spon·si·ble

(ri-**spon**-suh-buhl) *adjective*

Being the cause of. *My sister always says I'm responsible for every mess.*

re•verse

(ri-**vurss**)

1. *verb* To change to the opposite position. *Tina reversed her opinion on the band when she heard their great new album.*
2. *verb* To turn something around, upside down, or inside out. *I got a stain on my shirt, so I reversed it and wore it inside out.*
3. *noun* The control in a vehicle that makes it go backward. *He put the forklift in reverse to back up.*

reverse

sac•ri•fice

(**sak**-ruh-fisse) *verb*

To give up. *I had to sacrifice my plans to help my brother with his homework.*

se•vere

(suh-**veer**) *adjective*

Very bad or serious. *Eric was in a severe car crash, but he survived.*

spe•cies

(**spee**-sheez) *noun*

One of the groups into which plants and animals are divided. *The lion and cheetah are two different species of cat.*

sta•tis•tic

(stuh-**tiss**-tik) *noun*

A number. *One statistic said that housing costs would go up in our town.*

sus•tain

(suh-**stayn**) *verb*

1. To suffer something. *My dog fell out a window, but he didn't sustain any injuries.*
2. To keep something going. *I can sustain a handstand for 11 minutes.*

tense

(**tenss**) *adjective*

Nervous. *I get tense when I'm around a lot of people.*

tone

(**tohn**) *noun*

A way of speaking that shows a certain feeling. *My dad's voice changes tone when he's angry.*

trem•ble

(**trem**-buhl) *verb*

To shake. *Did you feel the ground tremble during the earthquake?*

Verb Endings

The past-tense form of **tremble** is **trembled**. The present-tense form is **tremble**. Verb endings show when an action takes place. To show an action in the past, you often can add **–ed**. If a verb ends with the letter e, it is usually dropped before adding **-ed** or **–ing**.

trend

(**trend**) *noun*

A pattern of change over time. *This year's fashion trends are similar to the trends of the 1960s.*

u•nique

(yoo-**neek**) *adjective*

Special and one-of-a-kind. *My best friend gave me a unique handmade necklace.*

u•ni•ver•sal

(yoo-nuh-**vur**-suhl) *adjective*

Concerning all the members of a group or of the world. *It's a universal agreement at our school that the walls need to be painted.*

ut•ter

(**uht**-ur) *verb*

To speak or make a sound from your mouth. *I was so mad at Brian that I couldn't even utter his name.*

va•cant

(**vay**-kuhnt) *adjective*

Empty. *The city is going to build a stadium on the vacant lot.*

vault

(**vawlt**)

1. *noun* An underground chamber. *The queen was buried in a stone vault.*
2. *verb* To leap over something using your hands or a pole. *She can vault over a ten-foot bar.*

vault

How to Use the Reading Handbook

This handbook includes the comprehension skills that you mastered in the **rBook**. You can use these directions and charts to review what you know. You can also use them in your other classes, like social studies and science. They can help you understand a new article or story.

Main Idea and Details

The **main idea** is the most important point about a topic. **Details** are the facts that support the main idea. To find the main idea and details:

• Decide what the topic is. Find the main idea about the topic.

• Look for the details that support the main idea.

▶ Use this chart to identify a main idea and supporting details.

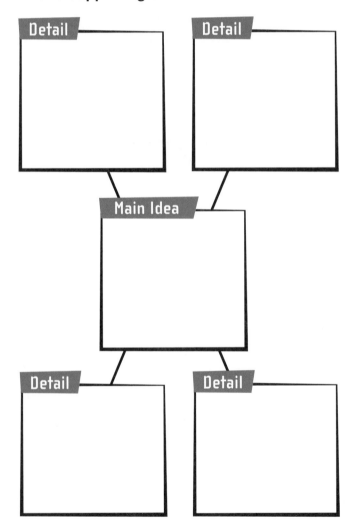

Sequence of Events

Sequence is the order in which events happen. To find the sequence of events:

- Try to remember the order in which events take place.

- Look for times, dates, and signal words, such as *first, then, next, after,* and *finally.*

- When you know the order, check it again. Make sure it makes sense.

► **Use this chart to identify a sequence of events.**

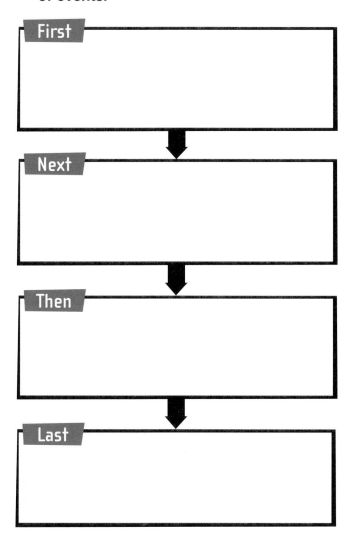

First

Next

Then

Last

Summarize

A **summary** is a short statement of the most important ideas in a reading. To summarize:

- Find the topic of the text.

- Look for the most important details about the topic.

- Restate the topic and important details in a short summary. Use your own words.

► **Use this chart to identify the topic and important details in a summary.**

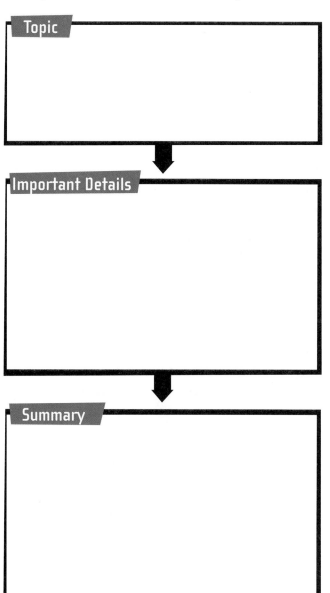

Topic

Important Details

Summary

Problem and Solution

A **problem** is a situation or event that causes trouble. A **solution** is what fixes the problem. To find the problem and the solution:

- Look for the problem.
- Look for attempts to solve the problem.
- Find the solution.

▶ **Use this chart to identify a problem and a solution.**

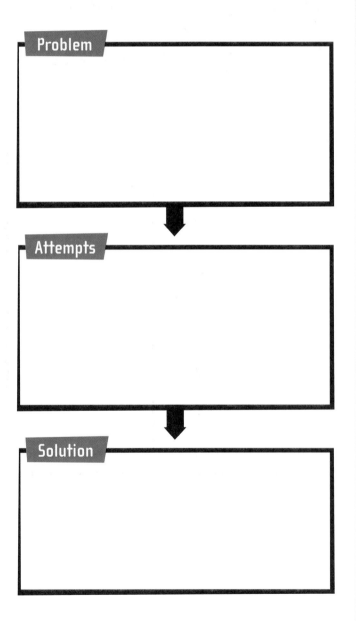

Cause and Effect

A **cause** is the reason something happens. An **effect** is the result of a cause. To find the cause and effect:

- Ask yourself "Why did it happen?" to find the cause.
- Ask yourself "What happened?" to find the effect.
- Look for signal words or phrases such as *because, so, as a result, therefore,* and *for this reason.*

▶ **Use this chart to identify cause-and-effect relationships.**

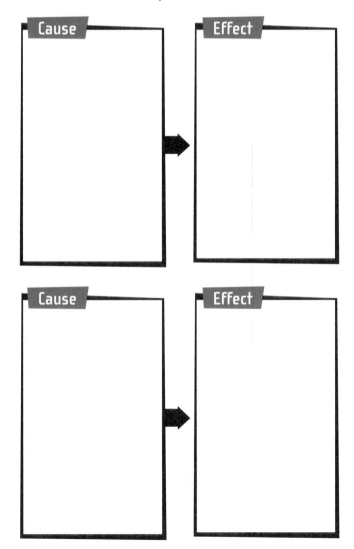

Compare and Contrast

When you **compare**, you tell how two things are the same. When you **contrast**, you tell how they are different. To compare and contrast:

- Ask yourself how two things are the same. Look for signal words such as *both, too, also,* and *in addition.*

- Ask yourself how two things are different. Look for signal words such as *but, rather than,* and *however.*

▶ **Fill in this chart to compare and contrast two elements in a reading.**

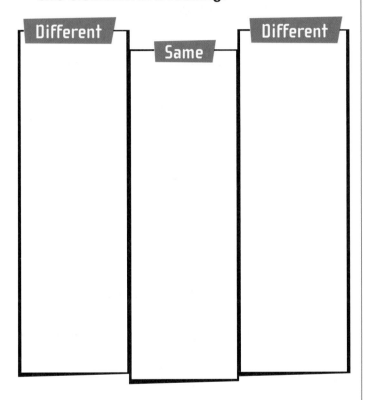

Different

Same

Different

Make Inferences

When you **make inferences**, you form ideas about things that are not directly stated in the text. To make inferences:

- Look for a situation in the text in which the author gives clues but doesn't state exactly what is happening.

- Think about what you already know about the topic.

- Combine the text clues with your own experiences or knowledge to make an inference.

▶ **Fill in this chart to make an inference.**

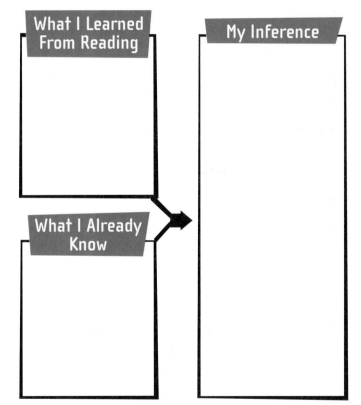

What I Learned From Reading

What I Already Know

My Inference

Story Elements

A short story is a brief piece of fiction. To understand a short story, look for four elements:

Setting

Setting refers to the place and time of a story. To analyze the setting:

- Look at the illustrations.

- Look for details that tell *where*. Ask yourself, "What words in the story help me imagine what the place looks like?"

- Look for story details that tell *when*. Ask yourself, "When does this story take place? Is it long ago, in the future, or the present?"

- Pay attention to any changes in the setting and how they affect the story.

Character

A character is a person or animal in a story. It's who the story is about. Often stories have several characters. We can identify the main characters because they are the ones the story is mostly about. Characters have special qualities, or traits, that make up their personalities. To analyze a character:

- Look for words the author uses to describe the character, especially adjectives.

- Pay attention to what the character thinks, says, and does.

- Be aware of what other characters say about the character.

- Think about what you already know about people and their behavior.

Plot

Plot refers to what happens in a story, including the problem, the events that lead to solving the problem, and the solution. To analyze the plot:

- Find out what the character's problem is.

- Look at how the character tries to solve the problem.

- Pay attention to what happens to help solve the problem. Look at what happens that gets in the way of solving the problem.

- Think about how the story turns out. Does the character solve the problem? How?

Theme

The theme is the message that the author wants you to take away from the story. It often helps you understand the author's purpose, thoughts, and feelings. To analyze theme:

- Think about what the characters do and say.

- Think about what happens to the characters.

- Ask yourself: What does the author want you to know about?

► Use this chart to keep track of the setting, character, plot, and theme of a story you are reading.

Story Title: _____			
	Part 1	**Part 2**	**Part 3**
Setting	Time: _____ _____ Place: _____ _____ _____	Time: _____ _____ Place: _____ _____ _____	Time: _____ _____ Place: _____ _____ _____
Character	Who is the main character? _____ Describe him/her: _____ _____ _____ _____	How does the character change? _____ _____ _____ _____ _____	What is the character like now? _____ _____ _____ _____ _____
Plot Events	What happens at the beginning of the story? _____ _____ _____ _____ _____	What happens in the middle of the story? _____ _____ _____ _____ _____	How does the story end? _____ _____ _____ _____
Theme	Author's message:		

Literary Terms

author a person who writes a short story, play, poem, novel, article, essay, or book

characters the people or animals in a story

concrete poetry poetry that has a shape that matches the meaning of the poem or a word in the poem

conflict an internal conflict takes place in the mind of a character who must resolve something. An external conflict takes place between two characters or between a character and a force of nature, society, or the unknown.

dialogue a conversation between characters

fiction an invented story

figurative language words used to say something other than their literal meaning, often to help the reader visualize what is happening. For example, "All the world's a stage."

flashback the return to an event that occurred before the present situation

foreshadowing hints of what is to come

historical fiction a story or novel whose setting is in some period in the past. Often real people from the past or important historical events are used in works of historical fiction.

imagery the use of vivid description to create pictures, or images, in the reader's mind

metaphor a comparison in which something is said to be something else. Metaphors use *is* or *was*. For example: He is a shining star.

mood the general feeling that an author creates. Mood is created largely through description and setting.

narrator the teller of a story. A first-person narrator tells a story using the word "I."

nonfiction writing about real people and factual events

novel a book-length piece of fiction that usually has a plot and deals with human experience

onomatopoeia the use of a word that sounds like the thing it stands for, such as *buzz* and *sizzle*

personal narrative a true story about a person's life told in the first person

photo essay a collection of photos and words that tells a story

plot what happens in a story, including the problem, the events that lead to solving the problem, and the solution

plot twist a turn of events in the story, novel, or play that is unexpected

poetry literature that uses language chosen for its sound and for its ability to express and evoke emotion

point of view the point from which the story is told. In the **first-person point of view,** the narrator is usually a character in the story. This narrator tells the story by using the pronouns *I* or *we.* In the **third-person point of view,** the narrator may or may not be a character in the story. This narrator uses the pronouns *he, she,* or *they.* Sometimes the narrator in the third-person point of view seems to know what every character is thinking and feeling. This narrator is called *omniscient,* or *all-knowing.*

repetition words, phrases, or sentences that are used over and over again

rhyme two or more words that have ending syllables with the same sound

rhythm a regular, repeated pattern of sounds in music or poetry

setting the time and place of a story

short story a brief piece of fiction

simile a comparison of two unlike things, using the words *like* or *as.* For example: She was as sweet as candy.

stanza a group of two or more lines in a poem that are printed as a unit and held together by length, rhyme scheme, and meter

suspense a state of uncertainty that keeps a reader reading

symbol something that has meaning in itself, but also stands for something else. For example, in a story, a heart may also stand for love.

theme the message that the author wants you to take away from the story. The theme is conveyed by the whole story—by the title, the plot, the characters, the setting, and the mood.

How to Use the Writing Handbook

This handbook includes the writing skills that you mastered in the **rBook**. You can use these directions and charts to review what you know. You can also use them to help you with a new writing assignment.

Expository Paragraph

An **expository paragraph** provides information and explains it.

- State the **topic** in the first sentence.
- Use **details** to support or explain the topic.
- Arrange the details in a **logical order**.
- Use **linking words** to connect the ideas.
- **Sum up** or restate the topic in the last sentence.

▶ **Use this chart to plan an expository paragraph.**

> **Topic Sentence**
>
> _____

> **Detail 1**
>
> _____

> **Detail 2**
>
> _____

> **Detail 3**
>
> _____

> **Conclusion**
>
> _____

Expository Summary

A **summary** gives the most important ideas and details from a reading.

- State the **topic of the reading** in the first sentence.
- Include only **important details**.
- Connect the details with **linking words**.
- **Use your own words** in the summary.
- Make sure your summary is **brief, yet complete**.

▶ **Use this chart to plan an expository summary.**

Topic Sentence

Detail 1

Detail 2

Detail 3

Detail 4

Persuasive Paragraph

A **persuasive paragraph** tries to convince the reader to share the writer's opinions.

- State your **opinion** clearly in the first sentence.
- Support your opinion with several **reasons**.
- Make sure that your reasons are **strong and convincing**.
- Use **linking words** to connect your reasons.
- **Restate** your opinion in a concluding sentence.

▶ **Use this chart to plan a persuasive paragraph.**

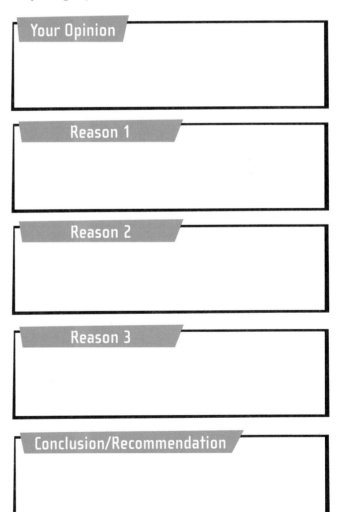

Your Opinion

Reason 1

Reason 2

Reason 3

Conclusion/Recommendation

Narrative Paragraph

A **narrative paragraph** tells a story about an event.

- State the **event** in the beginning.
- Use **details** to tell about the event.
- Arrange the details in the **time order** that they happened.
- Use **linking words** to connect the details.
- **Sum up** the event and tell your feelings about it in the ending.

▶ **Use this chart to plan a narrative paragraph.**

Event

Detail 1

Detail 2

Detail 3

Ending

Descriptive Paragraph

A **descriptive paragraph** describes a person, place, thing, or event by using interesting and specific details.

- State **what is being described** in the beginning.
- Use **descriptive details** about the subject.
- Make the details as **interesting** as possible.
- Use **linking words** to connect the details.
- **Sum up** the description and your **feelings** about it in the ending.

▶ **Use this chart to plan a descriptive paragraph.**

Topic Sentence

Detail 1

Detail 2

Detail 3

Conclusion

Literature Response

In a literature response, a reader relates a piece of literature to his or her life.

- **Relate your experience** to the main character's experience in the beginning.
- Use **details** to describe that experience.
- Arrange the details in the **time order** they happened.
- Use **linking words** to connect the details.
- **Sum up** your ideas and feelings with the ending.

▶ **Use this chart to plan a literature response.**

Introduce the Topic

Detail 1

Detail 2

Detail 3

Conclusion

Literature Review

A literature review presents the reviewer's opinion of a story.

- State **your opinion** of the story in the beginning.
- Include specific **reasons** that support your opinion.
- Make sure that your reasons are **strong and convincing.**
- Use **linking words** to connect the ideas.
- **Sum up** your opinion with the ending.

▶ **Use this chart to plan a literature review.**

Statement About the Story

Example or Reason 1

Example or Reason 2

Example or Reason 3

Concluding Statement

Grammar

▶ IDENTIFYING SENTENCES AND FRAGMENTS

A **sentence** is a group of words that tells a complete idea.

- The **subject** tells who or what the sentence is about.
- The **predicate** tells what someone or something does.

A **sentence fragment** is an incomplete sentence that can't stand by itself. Often, a fragment is missing either a subject or a predicate.

Example

Subject	Predicate
Irene's parents	moved to America from Mexico.
My neighbors	are from China and Vietnam.

▶ CORRECTING SENTENCE FRAGMENTS

A sentence fragment is an incomplete sentence. Often, sentence fragments are missing a subject or a verb. To fix some fragments, add a subject or verb to make a complete sentence.

Example

Sentence Fragment	Complete Sentence
A tornado our town today. [missing verb]	A tornado **struck** our town today.
Brought the tree down. [missing subject]	**A storm** brought the tree down.

To correct some sentence fragments, you can connect the fragment to a complete sentence by adding a comma and any missing words.

Example

Sentence and Fragment	Complete Sentence
A tornado struck our town today. Touched down in Texas.	A tornado struck our town today, and then it touched down in Texas.

▶ CORRECTING RUN-ON SENTENCES

A run-on sentence is made up of two complete thoughts that are incorrectly joined together.

- To fix a run-on sentence, separate the ideas into two **complete sentences**.
- Or, insert a comma and a connecting word between the thoughts.

Example

Run-on sentence:	Louisa lived here she ran away.
Complete sentences:	Louisa lived here. She ran away.
Complete sentence:	Louisa lived here, but she ran away.

▶ USING CORRECT VERB TENSE

The **tense** of a verb shows when the action happens.

- A present-tense verb shows action that is happening now.
- A past-tense verb shows action that took place in the past. Most past-tense verbs end in *-ed*.

Example

Present-Tense Verb	Past-Tense Verb
James works on a farm.	James worked on a farm last summer.
James picks fruit.	James picked fruit yesterday.

▶ USING IRREGULAR VERBS

Most past-tense verbs end in *-ed*. **Irregular verbs** do not.

- You must remember the different spellings of irregular past-tense verbs.
- The verb *to be* is a common irregular verb. Its present-tense forms are *I am, you are, he/she is*. Its past-tense forms are *I/he/she was, you/we/they were*.

Example

Present-Tense Verb	Past-Tense Verb
I am sorry for my actions.	I was sorry for my actions.
Amy sends out cards for birthdays.	She sent one to me last week.
They usually eat lunch at noon.	Yesterday, they ate lunch early.

▶ SUBJECT-VERB AGREEMENT

The **subject and verb** in a sentence must agree in number.

- A singular verb tells what one person, place, or thing is doing. It usually ends in *-s* or *-es*.
- A plural verb tells what more than one person, place, or thing is doing. It usually does not end in *-s* or *-es*.

Example

Singular Subject and Verb	Plural Subject and Verb
A noise comes from below.	The noises come from below.
Usher closes the door to the vault.	We close the door to the vault.

▶ USING SUBJECT AND OBJECT PRONOUNS

A **pronoun** is a word that takes the place of a noun in a sentence.

- Use a subject pronoun in the subject of a sentence.
- Use an object pronoun after a verb or after a word such as *for* or *to*.

Example

Subject Pronoun	Object Pronoun
I never liked snakes.	Snakes have always scared me.
We want to leave the island.	Snakes are too gross for us.
She found two in the house.	One snake almost bit her.
They are just creepy.	My sister and I hate them.

▶ USING ADJECTIVES THAT COMPARE

An **adjective** is a word that tells about or describes a noun. Adjectives can help compare two or more people or things.

- To use an adjective to compare two things, add *-er* to the adjective or use the word *more*.
- To use an adjective to compare three or more things, add *-est* to the adjectives or use the word *most*.

Example

Adjective Comparing Two Things	Adjective Comparing Three or More Things
Ekiwah is happier than he was before.	He is the happiest boy in the world.
Ekiwah is more famous than his friend.	He is the most famous writer his age.

▶ USING ADVERBS

An adjective describes a person, place, or thing. An adverb describes a verb, an adjective, or another adverb. Many adverbs end in *-ly*.

- Use an adverb to make your writing more precise.

Example

Adjective	Adverb
I walked home at a slow pace.	I slowly walked home.
Crazy Johnny was not a patient person.	I waited patiently for Crazy Johnny.
A quick pain shot through my legs.	The pain shot quickly through my legs.

Usage and Mechanics

► USING END PUNCTUATION

Different kinds of sentences use different **end punctuation marks**.

- A statement always ends with a period.
- A question always ends with a question mark.

Example

Statement	Question
I'm from Mexico.	Where are you from?
We are a nation of immigrants.	Were your parents immigrants?

► USING CAPITALS

Some words begin with a **capital letter**.

- The first word in a sentence begins with a capital letter.
- A proper noun begins with a capital letter.

Example

Correct	Incorrect
Lightning struck the building.	lightning struck the building.
The storm flooded Emily's home.	The storm flooded emily's home.

► USING CORRECT WORD ORDER

The **order of words** in a sentence must make sense.

- An adjective comes before the noun it describes.
- A helping verb comes just before the main verb in a statement.

Example

Correct	Incorrect
Louisa bought a new coat.	Louisa bought a coat new.
I know where Louisa is going.	I know where is Louisa going.

▶ USING COMMAS IN A SERIES

Items in a series are separated by **commas**.

- A series is a list of the same kinds of words.
- Commas follow every item in the series except the last one.

Example

Correct	Incorrect
Snakebites, cuts, and other injuries are part of the job.	Snakebites cuts and other injuries are part of the job.

▶ USING COMMAS WITH INTRODUCTORY WORDS

A **comma** follows an opening word or phrase at the beginning of a sentence.

- *Yes*, *No*, *Next*, and *Later* are examples of opening words.
- *In addition* and *After a while* are examples of opening phrases.

Example

Correct	Incorrect
Next, Kim began helping others. After a while, she felt better.	Next Kim began helping others. After a while she felt better.

▶ USING POSSESSIVES

A **possessive noun** shows ownership.

- Add an apostrophe (') and an -*s* to a singular noun.
- Add an apostrophe to a plural noun that ends in -*s*.

Example

Correct	Incorrect
Poe's story scared me. The friends' voices were low.	Poes story scared me. The friends voices were low.

▶ AVOIDING DOUBLE NEGATIVES

Negatives are words that express *no* or *not*.

- Use only one negative word to express a single negative idea.
- It is incorrect to use two negatives to express a negative idea.

Example

Correct	Incorrect
Tigers should never be pets.	Tigers shouldn't never be pets.
The snake didn't eat anything.	The snake didn't eat nothing.

▶ USING QUOTATION MARKS

Quotation marks show the exact words of a speaker.

- The first word of a quotation is capitalized.
- Punctuation usually goes inside the ending quotation mark.

Example

Correct	Incorrect
Lisa yelled, "Way to go!"	Lisa yelled, "way to go!"
Josue said, "You did it!"	Josue said, "You did it"!

rBook Workshop Log

▶ Fill in the date that you start and complete each Workshop. Rate your effort on a Workshop using the Rating Guide. Then answer a final question.

Rating Guide			
weak	okay	good	great
①	②	③	④

WORKSHOP 1  **The New Americans**

Date Started	Date Completed

Self-Assessment
Rate your effort during this Workshop.
① ② ③ ④

Which was your favorite article in this Workshop?

❑ "School Before Soccer"
❑ "Fitting In"
❑ "A New Immigration Boom"

WORKSHOP 2  **When Disaster Strikes**

Date Started	Date Completed

Self-Assessment
Rate your effort during this Workshop.
① ② ③ ④

Which type of natural disaster would you *least* want to be caught in?

❑ a lightning storm
❑ a forest fire
❑ a hurricane

Why? _____

_____

WORKSHOP 3 **Identity Crisis**

Date Started	Date Completed

Self-Assessment
Rate your effort during this Workshop.
① ② ③ ④

Do you think that Louisa got what she deserved? Why or why not?

_____

_____

_____

WORKSHOP 4 **Stolen Childhoods**

Date Started	Date Completed

Self-Assessment
Rate your effort during this Workshop.
① ② ③ ④

What will you remember most about this Workshop?

_____

_____

_____

_____

WORKSHOP 5 — Under Pressure

Date Started	Date Completed

Self-Assessment
Rate your effort during this Workshop.
① ② ③ ④

Who feels the most pressure at your school?

_____

_____

_____

WORKSHOP 6 — Poe: The Master of Horror

Date Started	Date Completed

Self-Assessment
Rate your effort during this Workshop.
① ② ③ ④

What was the creepiest part of "The Fall of the House of Usher" for *you*?

❑ Madeline Usher ❑ the storm

❑ the burial vault ❑ the house

Other: _____

_____

WORKSHOP 7 — Alien Invaders

Date Started	Date Completed

Self-Assessment
Rate your effort during this Workshop.
① ② ③ ④

Which alien invader would you least want in your neighborhood?

❑ kudzu ❑ brown tree snakes

❑ fire ants ❑ snakehead fish

Why? _____

_____

WORKSHOP 8 — Turning Points

Date Started	Date Completed

Self-Assessment
Rate your effort during this Workshop.
① ② ③ ④

Which teens in this Workshop would you want to meet in person?

❑ Jonathan Fong ❑ Waila and Dali

❑ Ekiwah Belendez Adler

Why? _____

_____

WORKSHOP 9 — The Streets of Harlem

Date Started	Date Completed

Self-Assessment
Rate your effort during this Workshop.
① ② ③ ④

Which reading did you like the best in this Workshop?

❑ "Heartbeat of Harlem," the article

❑ the story from *Bad Boy,* by Walter Dean Myers

❑ the poems by Langston Hughes

Topic Software Log

▶ Use these pages to keep track of the Topic CDs you have completed. Check off each segment you finish. Then answer a final question about each CD.

Topic CD 1
Art Attack

- ☐ 1.1 Crop Art
- ☐ 1.2 Halls of Fame
- ☐ 1.3 Young at Art
- ☐ 1.4 STOMP

My favorite segment was _____

_____

_____

Topic CD 4
Help Wanted

- ☐ 4.1 Jump Shot
- ☐ 4.2 In the Funnies
- ☐ 4.3 Building Dreams
- ☐ 4.4 Blast Off!

The job that I learned about and want the most is

_____

_____

Topic CD 2
Disaster!

- ☐ 2.1 Flood!
- ☐ 2.2 Earthquake!
- ☐ 2.3 Avalanche!
- ☐ 2.4 Volcano!

I would recommend this Topic CD to _____

_____

_____

Topic CD 5
Show Me the Money!

- ☐ 5.1 Making Money
- ☐ 5.2 Bogus Bills
- ☐ 5.3 Fighting Forgery
- ☐ 5.4 Mangled Money

One new thing I learned was _____

_____

Topic CD 3
Survive

- ☐ 3.1 Braving Alaska
- ☐ 3.2 Out of the Dust
- ☐ 3.3 In Search of Rain
- ☐ 3.4 Take a Dive

The most interesting thing I saw on this Topic

CD was _____

_____

Topic CD 6
You and the Law

- ☐ 6.1 Ban the Boards
- ☐ 6.2 What Curfew?
- ☐ 6.3 No Passing
- ☐ 6.4 Taking Mom to the Mall

One law I think should change is _____

_____

_____

Topic CD 7
Beating the Odds
- ☐ 7.1 Feel the Beat
- ☐ 7.2 Second Chance
- ☐ 7.3 Little Rock Nine
- ☐ 7.4 Write Direction

The person in this Topic CD I'd most like

to meet is _____

_____

Topic CD 10
Tales of Adventure
- ☐ 10.1 *The Call of the Wild*
- ☐ 10.2 Deep Freeze
- ☐ 10.3 Man With a Mission
- ☐ 10.4 On Top of the World

The most interesting person I learned about

was _____

_____

Topic CD 8
Extreme Sports
- ☐ 8.1 Extreme Snowboarding
- ☐ 8.2 Extreme Biking
- ☐ 8.3 Extreme Kayaking
- ☐ 8.4 Extreme Surfing

The extreme sport I'd most want to try is _____

_____

_____

Topic CD 11
First Person
- ☐ 11.1 A Timeless Voice
- ☐ 11.2 Sailing into History
- ☐ 11.3 Bringing Up Baldo
- ☐ 11.4 Daughter of a Legend

One new thing I learned was _____

_____

_____

Topic CD 9
The Whole World Watched
- ☐ 9.1 A Dark Day in Dallas
- ☐ 9.2 One Giant Leap
- ☐ 9.3 Freedom in South Africa
- ☐ 9.4 The People's Princess

The person I admire the most from this Topic

CD is _____

Topic CD 12
Scene Stealers
- ☐ 12.1 Prince of Salsa
- ☐ 12.2 Wrap Stars
- ☐ 12.3 Broadway for *Rent*
- ☐ 12.4 Wall to Wall

The art or performance I'd really like to see in

person is _____

_____

Book Log

▶ Use these pages to keep track of the books you read.

- Write the title in the blank box. Add a design if you like.

- Fill in the date that you started and completed each book.

- Mark what kind of book it was.

- Rate the book using the rating scale at right. Then write a statement about it.

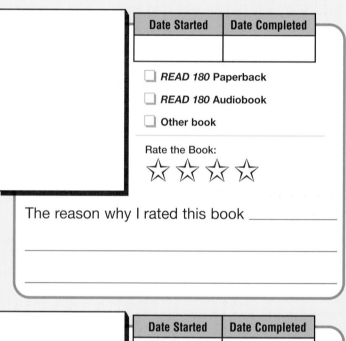

Rating Scale

It was great!	★★★★
It was good.	★★★☆
It was O.K.	★★☆☆
I didn't like it.	★☆☆☆

Date Started	Date Completed

☐ *READ 180* Paperback

☐ *READ 180* Audiobook

☐ Other book

Rate the Book:
☆ ☆ ☆ ☆

I would recommend this book to _____

_____

_____

Date Started	Date Completed

☐ *READ 180* Paperback

☐ *READ 180* Audiobook

☐ Other book

Rate the Book:
☆ ☆ ☆ ☆

The reason why I rated this book _____

_____

_____

Date Started	Date Completed

☐ *READ 180* Paperback

☐ *READ 180* Audiobook

☐ Other book

Rate the Book:
☆ ☆ ☆ ☆

This book reminded me of _____

_____

_____

Date Started	Date Completed

☐ *READ 180* Paperback

☐ *READ 180* Audiobook

☐ Other book

Rate the Book:
☆ ☆ ☆ ☆

I chose to read this book because _____

_____

_____

Date Started	Date Completed

☐ *READ 180* Paperback
☐ *READ 180* Audiobook
☐ Other book

Rate the Book:
☆☆☆☆

One question I have for the author is _____
_____
_____

Date Started	Date Completed

☐ *READ 180* Paperback
☐ *READ 180* Audiobook
☐ Other book

Rate the Book:
☆☆☆☆

I think I will/won't remember this book
because _____
_____

Date Started	Date Completed

☐ *READ 180* Paperback
☐ *READ 180* Audiobook
☐ Other book

Rate the Book:
☆☆☆☆

The best part of this book was _____
_____
_____

Date Started	Date Completed

☐ *READ 180* Paperback
☐ *READ 180* Audiobook
☐ Other book

Rate the Book:
☆☆☆☆

One new thing I learned in this book was _____
_____
_____

Date Started	Date Completed

☐ *READ 180* Paperback
☐ *READ 180* Audiobook
☐ Other book

Rate the Book:
☆☆☆☆

If I were making this book into a movie, it
would star _____
_____

Date Started	Date Completed

☐ *READ 180* Paperback
☐ *READ 180* Audiobook
☐ Other book

Rate the Book:
☆☆☆☆

This book was easy/hard to finish because
_____
_____

Date Started	Date Completed

☐ *READ 180* Paperback

☐ *READ 180* Audiobook

☐ Other book

Rate the Book:

☆ ☆ ☆ ☆

If I were making this book into a movie, it would star _____

_____

Date Started	Date Completed

☐ *READ 180* Paperback

☐ *READ 180* Audiobook

☐ Other book

Rate the Book:

☆ ☆ ☆ ☆

When I first saw this book, I thought it would be _____

_____

Date Started	Date Completed

☐ *READ 180* Paperback

☐ *READ 180* Audiobook

☐ Other book

Rate the Book:

☆ ☆ ☆ ☆

I'd recommend this book to _____

_____

Date Started	Date Completed

☐ *READ 180* Paperback

☐ *READ 180* Audiobook

☐ Other book

Rate the Book:

☆ ☆ ☆ ☆

Reading this book made me feel _____

_____

Date Started	Date Completed

☐ *READ 180* Paperback

☐ *READ 180* Audiobook

☐ Other book

Rate the Book:

☆ ☆ ☆ ☆

The most interesting thing about this book was _____

_____

Date Started	Date Completed

☐ *READ 180* Paperback

☐ *READ 180* Audiobook

☐ Other book

Rate the Book:

☆ ☆ ☆ ☆

One fact I learned in this book is _____

_____

Date Started	Date Completed

☐ *READ 180* Paperback

☐ *READ 180* Audiobook

☐ Other book

Rate the Book:

☆ ☆ ☆ ☆

The best thing about this book is_____

_____

_____

Date Started	Date Completed

☐ *READ 180* Paperback

☐ *READ 180* Audiobook

☐ Other book

Rate the Book:

☆ ☆ ☆ ☆

Three words that describe this book are _____

_____

_____

Date Started	Date Completed

☐ *READ 180* Paperback

☐ *READ 180* Audiobook

☐ Other book

Rate the Book:

☆ ☆ ☆ ☆

I would recommend this book to _____

_____

_____

Date Started	Date Completed

☐ *READ 180* Paperback

☐ *READ 180* Audiobook

☐ Other book

Rate the Book:

☆ ☆ ☆ ☆

This book should/should not have a sequel

because_____

_____

Date Started	Date Completed

☐ *READ 180* Paperback

☐ *READ 180* Audiobook

☐ Other book

Rate the Book:

☆ ☆ ☆ ☆

If I were making this book into a movie, it

would star_____

_____

Date Started	Date Completed

☐ *READ 180* Paperback

☐ *READ 180* Audiobook

☐ Other book

Rate the Book:

☆ ☆ ☆ ☆

One new thing I learned in this book is _____

_____

_____

Keep Track of Your Success!

▶ Create a bar graph showing your SRI Lexile scores over the year.

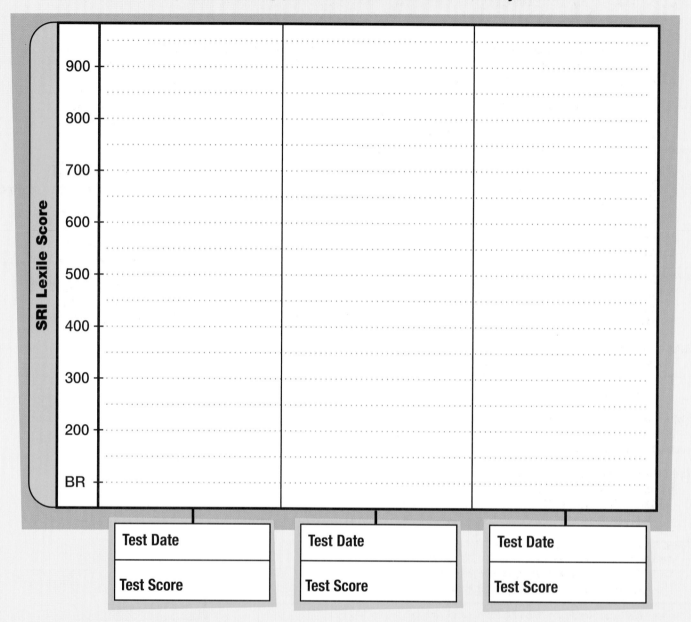

Test Date	Test Date	Test Date
Test Score	Test Score	Test Score

▶ Use this chart to keep track of your *READ 180* rSkills test scores.

	Test 1	Test 2	Test 3	Test 4	Test 5
Test Date					
Test Score					